The Magical Lore of Cats

Marion Davies

CAPALL BANN PUBLISHING

The Magical Lore of Cats

ISBN 1 898307 66 0

Internal illustrations by the author
Cover design by Daryth Bastin
Cover illustration by Sue Mason

Published by:

Capall Bann Publishing
Freshfields
Chieveley
Berks
RG20 8TF

To Bastet's children, with love

CONTENTS

INTRODUCTION

My first friend was a cat. I was three years old and having no other children to play with, my parents gave me a kitten as a companion. To this day I can remember her arrival: a spitting handful of Persian tortoiseshell fury. She stood on the dining room carpet, back arched and tail like a Christmas tree; outraged dignity in such a tiny body. Sally, as she came to be called, was born on a pile of potato sacks in a barn. Her first encounter with humanity was when she was taken from her mother, put in a pocket and deposited on our carpet. All cats know where they are well off and soon Sally accepted the love and hospitality of home. We were inseparable. She was one of the loveliest cats I have ever seen, Madame Puss, if ever there was one. She filled my solitary (but not lonely) days with her company and purred on my bed at night.

Unfortunately, at the age of six, we moved to a flat where animals were not permitted so Sally went to live with an elderly lady. I never forgot her, I don't think I have ever fully recovered from her loss. Since that time I have been owned by several cats, all distinct personalities, all greatly and equally loved, all sadly missed when their time came for them to pass on their way. But there was only one Sally.

A 'first cat' is similar to a 'first love'. It is unique and colours our attitude and perception towards all those who follow.

To those of us who love cats it is difficult to accept that there are many people whose feelings towards them are just the opposite. Indifference does not have a place in humanity's attitude to the cat, there is no middle road: we love 'em or hate 'em. Why does it stir up so many extreme emotions? What is the nature of this animal which has been worshipped as god and cursed as a devil? To find this out, we have to look at the history of man's association with the cat from the beginning of history.

The domestication of animals took place gradually. The arrangement was not as one-sided as it first appears. Domestication offered herd animals food, shelter and protection from predators. The dog (or it's ancestor, the wolf or jackal) was probably the first animal to form a partnership with man. Food, warmth and companionship appealed to his pack instinct and the dog moved to man's side, as his faithful servant and beloved companion - where he has been ever since. By guarding his master's home and lending his eyes and sense of smell to hunting expeditions, the dog gave man power over Nature.

With the beginnings of agriculture, (from about 8,500 B.C.E.) man gave up his nomadic ways and built settlements. Wild sheep and goats were confined for an easily accessible source of meat, clothing and milk. Still later, cattle were domesticated and by 6,500 B.C.E. were used as plough animals. Domestic animals became a form of currency, introducing the concept of wealth and status. In many parts of the world, they still are. Man learned to acquire wealth.

A great step forward came with the horse, without which 'history' may never have happened and the world would be very different today. The horse enabled man to travel quickly, move his possessions, go to war on a large scale, conquer his neighbour and build empires. The horse enabled man to widen his horizons and build empires.

The cat came lately to this scene and, like the dog, saw an opportunity and exploited it. However, unlike the dog, the cat is not a pack animal and therefore does not seek a leader and saw no reason to cultivate man's favour. With civilisation came granaries and kitchens - and rodents. The cat moved in, but under it's own terms. It came and went as it pleased. It is this aspect of choice which sets it apart from other domesticated animals. By giving up freedom for the benefits of domestication, other animals helped man to material gain and power: comfort and security are sweet enslavement.

Through the ages the cat has kept her integrity and challenges us to keep ours. Fear of the cat is the fear of making a decision or choice, of exposing our true natures for good or ill. It is far more comfortable to go along with the majority, even if you secretly feel they may be wrong. 'The Cat Who Walks Alone' certainly needs all of her nine lives, and deserves our respect.

The cat has a dual nature: the gentle, loving bundle which purrs on your lap is also the predator who murders the birds in your garden (all the more distressing if they were eating the scraps which you provided for them). This duality of nature is shared by man. All choices involve the decision to pass across boundaries. From the bridges built by the Devil, the eating of the fruit of the Tree of Life, to the breaking down of the hymen in the marriage bed, all are irrevocable choices. There is no turning back. Nothing comes free to us on this plane of existence, decisions (boundaries) taken bring with them debts which we must not, at our peril, disclaim. (Only man seeks a scapegoat for his 'mistakes'). Innocence is the price of choice, knowledge and responsibility are its rewards.

It is perhaps difficult, from our twentieth century hi-tech culture to understand why man worshipped animals. The answer is not as simple as may first be imagined. Ancient Egypt, in which the veneration of animals reached a sophisticated level, was only one culture to do this. The priesthood looked behind the animal form and saw qualities in its nature or behaviour which were admired, thus the animal became an archetype for instruction and understanding. Deities who were not depicted in animal form, generally had a sacred animal which epitomised their attributes. This is still seen today in the Christian religion wherein Christ is referred to as the 'Lamb of God'.

In view of our multi-cultural society, I have used the terms C.E. (Current Era) and B.C.E. (Before Current Era). instead of A.D. and B.C. By so doing, I mean no disrespect to any faith.

I love cats and hope you do as well. For this reason I have omitted certain material which is either very distressing or which may be used to do them harm. The cat has survived man's company for thousands of years. During the last two centuries, the cat's popularity has increased and this year statistics show that it has passed that of the dog.

Animals are precious and they will teach us much, if we allow them to do so. This is especially true of the cat, Bastet's child.

CHAPTER 1

EGYPT - RELIGION AND THE CAT

Worship of the cat has been found in many cultures world-wide, but it was in Ancient Egypt that it flourished to become the religion of the Pharaohs. The period lasted some three thousand years, from it's beginning as a tribal fetish to it's dissolution towards the end of the third century C.E. with the coming of Christianity as the state religion of Rome.

Dissolution, however, does not imply annihilation. The beliefs have echoed down through the ages where they have found expression for good or ill to the present time.

The intricate web of Egyptian religion is not easy to unravel. Attempting to make everything fit into a neat pattern, a task beloved by the Greeks, is almost impossible.

Time, geography and politics all confuse confusion even further.

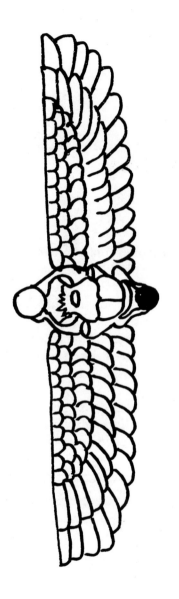

Winged Scarab

Originally, Egypt was two lands, divided into areas called 'nomes'. These corresponded roughly to our ancient tribal lands or modern counties. Each had it's patron deity with his or her symbol of a sacred animal or fetish carried on a pole. This served as a rallying point for members in war or large gatherings and was an object of honour. The Egyptian pantheon derives from these - any deities which were adopted from other cultures did not have their emblems mounted on a pole.

Just before the dynastic period, (c2900 B.C.E.), there was an influx of people from Asia Minor. Upper and Lower Egypt were brought together under one ruler, Hor-Aha, Narmer or as he is commonly known, Menes. With this ruler, Egypt saw the rise of an aristocracy and royal family. This set the scene for the political structure which ended with the death of Cleopatra and subsequent Roman rule in the first century, C.E.

These events played havoc with the existing religious system: nomes merged and understandably, no group was prepared to forsake a much-trusted deity for the sake of simplicity. The ruling classes brought their own religious ideas, resulting in two distinct pantheons: those in animal form or who had animal attributes and others in human form with cosmic (sky, sun, moon) qualities. The latter became 'supreme' whilst the local deities became their daughters, wives and offspring (or devils, depending on how much political upheaval was incurred).

Myths were adopted by one deity after another and edited by the priesthood to suit the circumstances. The Egyptians did not appear to be troubled by such inconsistencies, so although the central theme of the myths is constant, they all have variations.

Cat worship began c2,700 B.C.E. during the age of Taurus, the period which marked the flourishing of agriculture. Cattle became important for meat and/or milk and leather, as draught animals and for barter. In recognition of this worth, deities with bovine form or attributes came into being: Hathor, the Egyptian mother goddess, The Apis bull in Memphis, the Minotaur of Crete, the Golden Calf of Exodus, and the rites of Attis and Mithra, to mention but a few. Spanish bull-fighting is a legacy of the age.

The African Wild Cat (Felis lybica) is a desert-living animal, with markings very similar to our modern tabbies. Unlike the Wild Cat of north-west Europe, this cat is relatively amicable to man. With the rise of agriculture, rodents saw a 'free meal' of grain and the cat saw a 'free meal' of rodents in the granaries. The Egyptians consumed vast quantities of grain and beef and beer, so protection of the granaries was vital to survival of man and beast. When Puss moved in, it endeared itself not only by protecting the precious corn but also by killing poisonous snakes which were a hazard. The cat earned for itself a place in man's affections - for a while, at least.

The Rise of the Cat

The love of the Egyptians for their cats is found throughout the land. The earliest known picture of a cat, shown wearing a collar, dates from c2600B.C.E

A stela now in the Ashmolean Museum shows two cats, one addressed as 'The Great Lady Cat' and the other as, 'The Beautiful Lady Cat'. It is also inscribed with hymns to Ra who is called, 'The Great Tomcat'. Yet another stela, from Deir-el-Medina has the inscription, 'The Beautiful and Gracious Cat'.

Another stela, dating from the eleventh century, B.C.E. shows a fat cat crouching under it's owner's chair. Cats are often shown sitting beneath or beside the mistress' chair. They are never seen by the master's chair and this shows a similarity to the pictures of Diana and Artemis who are also have cats sitting at their feet.

Pictures in tombs also portray the cat in hunting scenes flushing out wildfowl: a task now performed by dogs.

Many cats were mummified and placed in tombs. Prince Tuthmosis had his cat's body placed in a sarcophagus. An inscription shows her as sitting at a table receiving offerings while her mummified form stands behind her. The inscription reads 'Osiris, the Lady Cat'. At Abydos a twelfth century pyramid contained a chamber with seventeen cats, complete with bowls for their use in the afterlife. Even the poorest of people would do all they could to give their cat a decent burial. Owners went into deep mourning and shaved their eyebrows.

To kill a cat was punishable by death. Diodorus Siculus tells of a Roman who killed a cat. Despite the intervention of Egyptian officials, the crowd murdered him.

Veneration for the cat has even led to Egyptian defeat in war. During the reign of Psammetichus III (525B.C.E), Persian invaders laid siege to the city of Pelusium, close to what is now modern Port Said. The Persians, under Cambyses II, rounded up as many cats as they could find and released some on the battlefield and others were carried by the soldiers. The Egyptians refused to fire, lest a sacred cat be hurt. Defeat was disastrous. The rulers of the following dynasty (twenty-seventh) were Persian.

If a house was burning, the first thought was to save the cats. Unfortunately, seeing rows of people standing by the door, the terrified animals usually turned and ran straight back into the flames.

Little girls were called 'Mai-Sheri' as a term of endearment. The name means 'Pussy' or 'Sweety'.

Bastet

The home of Amu-Khent was later the city of Bubastis. It is now the modern Tall Basta, situated near Zagazik in the Eastern Delta of Lower Egypt. Bubastis was an important centre in the Delta region from early times as its situation on several arms of the Nile made it a centre for travel and the transport of goods. The whole city was dedicated to cat-worship as seen in the scores of wall-paintings, sculptures and papyri from the area.

The goddess of Bubastis is Bastet. In the early days of her worship, Bastet was depicted as being lion-headed, like many other Egyptian goddesses with whom she is equated/confused. From about 1000 B.C.E. onwards her image gradually becomes cat-headed, although some statues in her temples often remained lion-headed. Her earlier image was not forgotten, for during her celebrations in the month of May, it was considered disrespectful to hunt lions.

Bastet is the daughter of the sun god, Ra and she is often described as 'the Rage of his Eye' (other goddesses also have this title). Texts recounting battle scenes describe the defeated falling like the 'victims of Bastet'. When Ra became merged with Amun of Thebes, Bastet was considered to be the eldest daughter of Amun. In later

Bastet

times, she became the daughter of Osiris. In each case her mother is Isis. Bastet has a son, the lion-headed Maahes.

Construction of a temple to Bastet, was begun in the reign of Cheops during the fourth dynasty (c2613-2494 B.C.E.). Statues and effigies of Bastet show her holding a sistrum, an aegis and a basket over one arm. Very often kittens sit at her feet. Early inscriptions term her as 'Lady of Life'. Bastet was also worshipped in the temple at Karnak.

The first ruler of the twenty-second dynasty (c935-730 B.C.E.), Sheshonq I, made Bubastis his capital around the year 945B.C.E. Pharaohs of this dynasty added the epithet, 'Son of Bastet' to their names to show their allegiance.

A later ruler, King Osorkon II had a magnificent temple built to Bastet enlarging on the earlier building. A red granite square was surrounded by canals, in the centre was an altar to the goddess, depicted as a white cat. This shrine was screened by a plantation of bushes, surrounded by a wall. The interior of the building was richly decorated with friezes and inscriptions. One of them shows King Osorkon II addressing Bastet: "To You I bow and offer all my lands' while another says, 'In You I recognise the power of Ra'. The temple must have been a labour of love, as red granite had to be transported by ship from the quarries of Upper Egypt at great expense.

Bubastis and the Bubastite dynasty are mentioned in the Old Testament. As neighbours, Israel and Egypt had commerce and disaffected Jews found refuge beyond the borders of Egypt. One such was Jeroboam who fled the wrath of king Solomon (who was himself married to an Egyptian princess).

'Solomon therefore sought to kill Jeroboam. And Jeroboam arose and fled into Egypt, unto Shishak king of Egypt, and was in Egypt until the death of Solomon'.

I Kings 11:v.40

Jeroboam returned when Rehoboam, Solomon's son became king. Rehoboam was a heartless man and civil war broke out. Jeroboam lead the breakaway faction and was eventually crowned also. Two kings cannot rule one country. Jeroboam was eventually overthrown and during the civil war which still raged, king Sheshonq (Shishak) invaded Israel:

'And it came to pass in the fifth year of king Rehoboam, that Shishak king of Egypt came up against Jerusalem: And he took away the treasures of the house of the Lord, and the treasures of the king's house: he even took away all: and he took away all the shields of gold which Solomon had made.'
I Kings 14:v 25-26

Perhaps king Shishak was avenging the death of his friend, Jeroboam.

In the temple at Karnak, there is a relief depicting this incident. The god Amun holds a sickle-like sword in his right hand and presents Sheshonq with over 150 shackled prisoners. Each prisoner represents a town or city which fell to the Egyptians.

The temple of Bastet is mentioned in the Old Testament in the book of Ezekiel 30 v17, under the name of Pi-beseth:

13

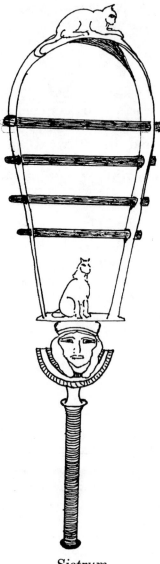

Sistrum

'The young men of Aven and of Pi-biseth shall fall by the sword: and these cities shall go into captivity'.

Bubastis was destroyed by Persian invaders about 350 B.C.E.

Bastet carries three symbols, mentioned earlier. The sistrum is an ancient rattle-like musical instrument. It is usually decorated with cats, but sometimes the handle depicts Hathor, the goddess with whom Bast is identified. Hathor has been said to be 'As merry as Bastet'. When the worship of Isis was carried to the Roman world, two paintings were discovered showing a cat sitting on a large sistrum. A priest of Isis and a kneeling woman appear to be shaking sistra before it. Temple dancers in Egypt carried sistra with cat effigies on them. As the goddess of pleasure, music and dance, Bastet is linked in Egyptian art with the gnome-like god Bes. Carvings show Bastet, Bes and sacred cats together. Bes is an interesting character, he is god of pleasure, fire and women in childbed. He is usually shown as a naked or semi-naked dwarf.

The basket links with the womb of life, in other cultures it takes the form of a cup, cauldron or bag which either never empties or restores the dead to life. Hence Bastet is a goddess of fertility and motherhood with Underworld associations.

The aegis resembles a small shield. Usually decorated with a lion or cat head. As it is an instrument of defence, the lion head reminds any protagonists that Bastet was originally lion-headed and is an aspect of the fierce Sekhmet. Mother-goddesses are often linked with war. The sistrum was an instrument which also summoned soldiers. Hathor and Bastet are no exceptions.

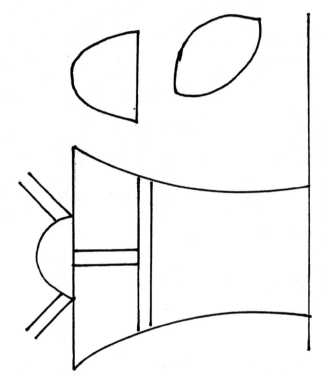

Hieroglyph of Bastet's Name

The Festival of Bastet took place in the month of May. The richly decorated and perfumed barges, sometimes bearing her statue passed along the Nile, accompanied by processions and music. Worshippers followed the barge in small boats, singing and making merry.

Bastet's celebrations were orgiastic, emphasising her fertility/pleasure aspect, with some women becoming hierodouloi for the duration of the celebrations. The historian Herodotus gives a description of the festival, remarking on the large numbers of worshippers who disembarked at each town along the way, enticing others to join them.

Mut, Amun their adopted son, Khonsu also had festivals on barges.

In common with other Goddesses of Life, Bastet had entrance to the Underworld. An amulet has been found bearing the inscription:

'May Bastet revivify the deceased among the glorified'.

and

'Hail Bast, coming forth from the secret place, I have not set my mouth in motion (against anyone)'.

The cat, as it represents choice of action, is at home in the Underworld where the choices made in life are weighed against the feather of justice.

There are some interesting descriptions of Bastet's dress and that of her priestesses. One of Bastet's titles is 'The Lady With The Red Clothes'. It appears that this title was also applied to her priestesses. Red is the colour of motherhood as well as pleasure. At Nemi there was a statue to Bastet together with a description of her dress:

'A robe of silk, purple and turquoise green.
A shirt of purple linen with two girdles, one gilt.
Two robes, two mantles.
A tunic and a white dress'.

A later statue of Bastet, dating from the twenty-sixth dynasty (c664-525 B.C.E.) shows a change in dress. The long, straight dress of Egyptian women is still worn, but is no longer of the plain linen material. It appears as if woven or embroidered in a herring-bone pattern. It could be the result of a foreign influence

What did Bastet represent to the Egyptians? As the mild sun, she ruled the growth of corn and crops. As the 'moon' eye of Horus, she was both a virgin goddess and a mother goddess. 'Virgin' in this context implies freedom from belonging to any one man. Through her father, Osiris, she was present in the Underworld. Some statuettes of Bast show her with the emblem feather of Ma'at in her ears. Ma'at is the goddess of truth and justice and the heart of each deceased person has to be weighed against this in the Underworld.

Equated with Hathor she ruled pleasure, as the daughter of Isis, she was All. For the ordinary people, though, Bastet represented pleasure, laughter and music. In this respect she certainly equates with the Roman Venus or Greek Aphrodite. Bastet's name is written in hieroglyphs as a jar of perfume.

The cult of Bast spread beyond Egypt. Phoenician inscriptions have been found saying 'Abd Bast' - the 'Servant of Bast' and 'Pa'ol Bast', 'Bast has made'. It is

18

understandable that the Phoenicians 'adopted' Bastet, as they were known to take cats aboard ship when they sailed on trading expeditions. If these were Egyptian cats, they must have been stolen. Theft of a cat was punishable by death, perpetrators were pursued relentlessly. It may have been the Phoenicians who first brought the domestic cat to Britain when they traded for tin. Though some authorities credit it's arrival with the Romans.

CHAPTER 2

CHILD OF THE SUN

Cats love warmth. They are at their happiest when curled up in sunshine on a hot summer's day or dozing in front of a cheery fire on cold, wet winter evenings. It is not surprising, coming as they do from Egypt where the sun shines relentlessly. The French writer Colette understood and loved cats. Read *'The Ganymede Cat'* from her book, *'Sept Dialogues des Betes'*. A cat addresses the fire as winter approaches. It is a perceptive piece of writing.

The symbol of the sun, as a circle with a dot in the centre appeared in pre-dynastic times (5000-3100 B.C.E.) and still represents the sun in modern astrology. Our western astrological sign of Leo equates the lion and royalty with the sun.

The glyph of the sign of Leo originally represented the tail of a lioness, which may reflect the status of women in Egypt at that time. Royal succession passing through the Great Royal Wife. The Sun God Ra equates with the sign of Leo. But Ra is the Great Cat, not a lion. The reason for this will be seen later.

Egyptian religion had several deities who were either cat-headed or were associated with cats of whom perhaps Bastet, mentioned in the previous chapter is best known. In view of the complexity of divine relationships, the situation will (hopefully) be simplified by a Divine Who's Who before discussing the mythology concerning Them.

Ra or Re

The cult of the sun-god, Ra, was established long before the two kingdoms united and continued throughout most of the dynastic period. He is depicted as a hawk-headed man or a cat. His centre was originally at Heliopolis, where, in the temple, the statue of a cat was inscribed to his daughters, Sekhmet and Bastet:

'Kindly is She as Bast. Terrible is She as Sekhmet'.

Under Menes, the capital was moved to Thebes where Ra merged with the incumbent Sun God, Amun. He was then called Amun-Ra.

Ra as deity of the sun traversed the sky in a boat and each morning battled with the serpent of darkness, Apep. Apep was an immortal force and battle was waged constantly with Ra always being victorious, but Apep never being exterminated. Together Ra and the serpent Apep symbolise the eternal struggle: light and dark, summer and winter, night and day. A never ending struggle, a quest for harmony and the reconciliation of opposites

The illustration overleaf shows Ra as the solar cat beheading the serpent by the Tree of Life, the Shoab or Persea tree.

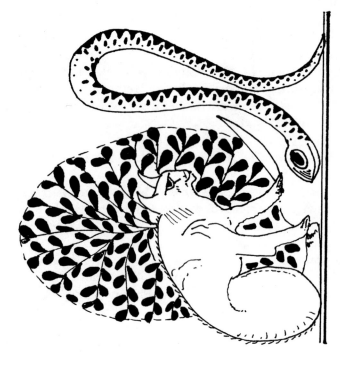

Ra as the solar cat beheading the serpent by the Tree of Life

From the Egyptian *'Book of the Dead'*, Ra affirms,

'I am the Great cat which fought hard by the Persea tree'.

Also:

'The male cat is Ra himself. He is called Mau by the words of Sa'

Sa is the personification of intelligence. The Egyptians therefore called the cat 'Mau'. It is a coincidence that the word is onomatopoeic as well as meaning 'to see' - the cat is the 'Eye of God'. The cult of Ra or Amun-Ra was materialistic. Entry to the afterlife was through wealth and status: therefore restricted to the royal family and selected nobles. No prayers to Ra have been found for the repose of the soul or mercy for wrongdoing. Status was enough to secure a place on Ra's ship of eternity in the heavens The cult of Ra finally gave way to that of Osiris, with it's added concept of an afterlife attainable by all.

Isis or Au-Set

Isis is the Great Mother and Example of Perfect Womanhood whose worship spread throughout the known world, even reaching the shores of Britain. Her name means 'Throne' or 'Seat' meaning that she is the basis of all things. She has many names, among them 'The Female Ra/Horus' and 'Stella Maris', the Star of the Sea.

She equates with many other Goddesses. She is provider of corn, Goddess of Moon and Earth. She is Mother, Physician and Counsellor. She has charge over the Dead and Magic. Isis is All. She is depicted as suckling the infant Horus

23

(which later gave rise to the pictures of 'Madonna and Child' in Christian art), or a woman wearing the solar disc between cow' horns (as does Hathor).

Bastet

Daughter of Ra and Isis. She is alternatively daughter of Osiris and Isis. Originally having the head of a lion, later became head of the cat. Her name means 'Soul of Isis', Ba-en-Auset'.

Greek inscriptions have been discovered on the islands of Ios and Andros. These proclaim Isis' attributes in Her own words: among them, *'For Me was built the city of Bubastis'*. Bastet has been identified with and equated with Hathor, Sekhmet, Neith, Diana, Artemis, Pakhet and Tefnut to name a few. Bastet is also the 'Eye of Ra'.

As daughter of Osiris, Bastet is Mistress of the Dead. She has a lion-headed son, Maahes by Ra. Maahes is God of Healing, He had a cult centre in Leontopolis and a sanctuary at Bubastis.

Sekhmet

Sekhmet is also the lion-headed daughter of Ra. She is the alter-ego or twin of Bastet and represents the fierce heat of the sun. Sekhmet is described as the 'Eye of Ra'. She is the wife of Ptah, the Creator god of Memphis. He is an aspect of Ra, personifying The Mind and Heart of Creation.

Sekhmet is associated with healing and has a lion-headed son, Nefertem, equated by the Greeks with Asculapeus.

Nefertem was the originally the God of primordial creation of Lower Egypt, where he was son of the Cobra-Goddess, Uadjyt.

Osiris

Osiris may have originally been a king and deified after his death. His cult centre was at Busiris. He is God of growing vegetation, fertility, the moon and the Underworld. Father of Bastet and Horus. Husband/brother of Isis.

Osiris was murdered by his brother, Set. The body was sealed in a coffin and cast into the Nile, where it came to rest at Byblos and became encased in a tree-trunk.
Isis retrieved the body and in the form of a sparrow-hawk, hovered above it, reviving it sufficiently to conceive Horus.

Set again found the body and hacked it into fourteen pieces which he scattered around Egypt. Isis found all but one piece, the genitals. She embalmed the body, helped by Set's wife, Nephthys. Osiris regained life as ruler of the Underworld, where, like other chthonic deities (Hades) he guards the seed corn and is supreme judge of the dead. All deceased Pharaohs become Osirises.

Horus

The son of Isis and Osiris, the Divine Son. Brother of Bastet. Horus became the chief deity of a group of clans when the kingdom united. (The incoming people of Menes were known as 'Shemsu-Hor', 'People of Horus'). A God of the sky, usually depicted with the head of a falcon. His face the sky, his right eye the sun and the left, the moon. He later became identified with the sun god and his cult was

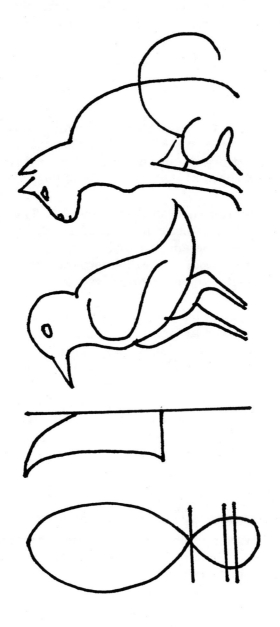

Egyptian Hieroglyph for Mau (Cat)

26

assimilated with that of Ra. His name then being Ra-Horakhty.

There is a myth that Horus struck off the head of Isis, his mother and replaced it with that of a cow. This indicates that the Horus people accepted Hathor as his mother and equated her with Isis.

Horus continued the struggle with Set on his father's behalf. Set tore out Horus' left eye and Horus castrated Set. Neith was called to act as arbitrator and gave Horus his father's inheritance and Set compensation. Horus became identified with the living Pharaoh and eventually merged with his father.

Set

Set is one of the oldest divinities of Egypt. At first Set was not evil: he was the essence of darkness, representing the abyss out of which the sun rose. It was during the political struggle for supremacy with incoming people that Set became the personification of Evil. Ancient legend tells that the South was given to Set and the north to Horus. Set's kingdom was then taken from him and also given to Horus. Thus the quarrel began.

Under the New Kingdom, (eighteenth to twenty-second dynasties), Set was replaced as the arch-enemy of Ra, by the Serpent which tried to prevent the sun rising each morning. Set was the twin of Osiris and brother of Isis. He was the uncle of Horus. Set was banished to the desert, a place of sterility, symbolised by injuries received from Horus.

Hathor

Hathor is described as 'Mother of her Father and Daughter of her Son'. Originally the Great Mother. She is the 'alternative' Mother of Horus and equated with Isis and Bastet. The name Hathor means 'House of Horus'. The term 'house' does not mean the womb but the sky. She is Lady of Heaven, Earth and the Underworld. She is kindly to the dead as well as the living. She leans from her sacred tree, the sycamore-fig and offers food to the dead. She was originally depicted as a cow or a cow-headed woman. Later statues show her with the horns of a cow. She, like Bastet, carries a sistrum. She is also called 'The Eye of Ra'.

Neith

Virgin Mother Goddess of Sais. Sais was the capital of Egypt during the twenty-sixth dynasty. Originally depicted as a cow. A sacred cat was kept in her temple. She equates with Hathor, Isis, and Bastet. Neith, like Hathor, offers refreshment to souls on their way to the Underworld.

Mut

The Mother-Goddess of Thebes. Wife of Amun. She is often depicted as having the head of a vulture. It was believed that male vultures did not exist and the females were impregnated by the south wind. The vulture is therefore symbolic of virginity. The cat and vulture were the sacred animals of Mut. Mut and Amun had an adopted son, Khensu, god of the moon. He was associated with healing.

Nut

Female principle of the waters which were before creation. Depicted with head of a serpent or (rarely) a cat.

Ma'at

Goddess of truth and justice. Her symbol is a feather which is weighed against the heart of the deceased in the Underworld. Some statues of Bastet show feather-like hairs in Her ears, equating her with Ma'at. Ma'at is also the Eye of Ra/Horus. The name Ma'at may also have connection with an Indo-Aryan word, 'mati', meaning 'Eye'.

Pakhet

A lion-headed Goddess. She is equated with Artemis at a cave called Speos Artemidos.

It is at the temple of Pakhet, that a large quantity of mummified cats were discovered at the end of the last century. They were shipped to Liverpool, where in the absence of suitable purchasers, they were ground to a powder and sold as fertiliser. Admittedly, the cat stands for fertility, but this sacrilegious act is surely taking things a bit too far!

In 1982, another cemetery containing mummified cats was found at Saqqara and Pakhet's temple at Beni Hasan. These were left to rest in peace.

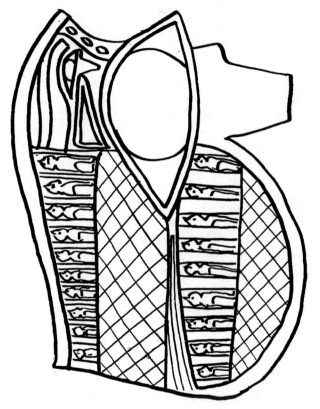

Sacred Eye inset with Nineteen Cats

Tefnut

Lion-headed Goddess known as the 'Ethiopian Cat'. She went to Nubia but Ra sent Thoth, God of Wisdom to bring her back. She is the Goddess of moisture, her absence may have marked a period of drought in the North.

The Eye of Ra

The Sacred Eye of Ra, or the Utchat, is considered a powerful talisman and is found engraved on tomb walls and carried as an amulet. Cats appear on utchats and utchats are engraved upon cat-amulets. Alone the utchat is a symbol of the Eye of God. When two appear together, very often on sarcophagi, it gives the deceased the protection of the deities of sun and moon. Because of it's great power, the Eye of the Sun was separated from the god and became a divinity in it's own right.

The following is the legend of the Eye. This legend (with variations) is also attributed to Atum, Osiris and Horus.

> In the beginning, the sun god had only one eye. When he wept, the tears which fell became the first man and woman. In time, these beings wandered away and the god became troubled. He sent his Eye to seek for them. In its absence, a second eye grew in its place.

> Eventually, the first eye returned, bringing the children and was enraged to see a usurper on the deity's forehead. The god tried to placate his angry eye by turning it into a cobra and placing it in his crown, where it became the uraeus.

The first eye was never appeased and became known as the raging heat of the sun, Sekhmet. The milder (second) eye became Bastet.

There is another legend concerning the Eye:

In time, the ageing sun god, Ra became aware that humanity was beginning to speak disrespectfully about him. He called the other gods to his presence and asked their advice. They said,

'The fear of thee is great. Let thine Eye go against those who are planning evil against thee'.

Ra dispatched his Eye in the form of the goddess, Hathor. She departed and slaughtered many. On return she confessed that the slaughter was pleasing to her. Once again she set out, this time in the form of the goddess Sekhmet. (some accounts say Hathor). Ra was horrified at what he had unleashed on humanity and gave orders that beer be mixed with the juice of pomegranates and poured before the angry Goddess. She drank the brew, saw her reflection and became intoxicated. Thus humanity was saved.

Bastet, Sekhmet, Hathor, Isis and Ma'at were known as the 'Eye of Ra'. Sekhmet, Hathor and rarely Bastet were also the 'Rage of his Eye'. (A subtle warning that even the gentlest of cats can scratch).

The Eye of Horus

The name Horus means 'he who is on high'. It was believed that the face of Horus was the sky. His left eye the moon (the 'mild' sun) and his right eye, the sun. The moon was created because the Eye of the sun god tended to stay out at night (like all cats, given the chance). The cat, with it's glowing eyes was considered to carry the sun's light throughout the night. When the cults of Ra and Horus became merged, both legends became interchangeable.

The two eyes of Horus also took on extra meaning: the left eye, corresponding to the feminine nature and therefore lunar, represented mental and physical well-being. The right eye represented human joy and vigour. Since both Bastet and Sekhmet have been described as the 'flaming eye of Horus', the Sacred Eye is always that of a cat.

The Uraeus

Why did Ra turn his Eye into a cobra? And how does this concern the cat? It is an attempt to merge two religious beliefs.

Let us take a look back to early times when the serpent-deity was all-powerful.

In prehistoric times, Egypt was two lands. The Lady of Upper (southern) Egypt was Nekhebt. Her principle was the vulture, 'mut'. Ancient belief held that there were no male vultures, therefore the females became pregnant by the south or south-east wind. Winds are associated with the serpent: all winds were thought to have the tails of snakes and live in caves high up in the mountains. Southern Egypt was mountainous. Nekhebet appears in human form, winged, holding a cobra-headed sceptre. The vulture head-dress was worn by the queen-mother, symbolising virginity in the sense that Queens of Egypt chose their husbands.

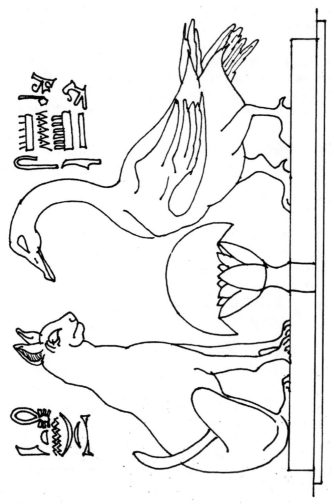

The cat associated with Mut and the goose associated with Amun.From a photograph in the possession of Hirmer Fotoarchiv.

34

The name, Mut, is found again when the two lands were united under Menes and she became the wife of Amun, sun god of Thebes. (Later Amun-Ra). The sacred animals of Mut are the cat, cow and vulture. She is identified with other virgin goddesses, Diana and Artemis. The illustration shows the symbols of Mut and Amun. Amun's sacred animal was the goose which was later replaced with the ram. The goose was the Earth Goose, the Great Cackler who laid the Cosmic Egg from which all Creation sprang. This is yet another Creation legend. (see illustration overleaf).

The corresponding goddess of Lower (northern delta) Egypt was Ua-Zet, 'Great Serpent'. (Variations of her name are: Uajyt, Uatchet, Uto, Buto, Udot and Per Uadjit). Some texts say that it was Hathor in serpent-form. It is probable that the name Au-Set is also Ua-Zet. If this is so, then Isis equates with Great Serpent.

There is a further connection when Isis taunts the aged Ra with serpents, forcing him to give her his secret name. Knowledge of a secret name bestowed great power. The word for 'eye' in Egyptian, is 'uzait' and is always written in the feminine form. It is very similar to, if not the same as the name of the serpent goddess above, Au-Set or Ua-Zet.

From c3000 B.C.E, the beginning of dynastic times, this serpent goddess became known as Nut - 'she who existed before creation'. Nut is usually seen as a woman whose body arches over the world. However, she has also been depicted as a woman with the head of a serpent or cat. She became identified with the mother-goddess Net, in whose temple at Sais was kept a sacred cat.

Just before 3000B.C.E., an incursion of foreigners entered Neolithic Egypt, uniting the two lands and marking the beginning of dynastic history. These invaders were called the Shemsu-Hor, bringing with them the male cosmic deity, Horus. These people took upon themselves the rulership of Egypt and marriage was kept within the royal family. Ua-Zet and the Vulture from the south were taken into 'protective custody' where they became symbols of the two crowns of Upper and Lower Egypt. The uraeus sat above the Pharaoh's head and the Vulture sat above the brow of the Queen Mother. The Uraeus was, as the Pyramid Texts state, magically guarded by the Pharaoh. (Some state that it was the Pharaoh who was guarded by the uraeus). When he died, the uraeus would try to escape if possible. The implication being that without the Pharaoh, the new political situation may not have been as stable as it might have been.

Ra's boat, emerging from primal waters, has a similarity to the Sumerian creator God, Enki. Enki also had to struggle with a great Serpent. Ra fought the 'serpent of darkness' known as Zet, later Apophis or Apep. The serpent of the primal waters and the 'resident' deity. Ra had to be a Great Cat: He had to overcome the serpent. Cats kill serpents. Lions do not.

The Scarab

Another creature associated with both the sun and the cat is the scarab (or dung) beetle. Many statues of cats have scarabs hanging from their necks and many scarabs have a cat inscribed upon them.

Like the vulture, the scarab was believed to reproduce itself from itself. Horapollo declared that there is a beetle which,

'Rolls the ball from east to west, looking himself toward the east. Having dug a hole, he buries it for twenty-eight days; on the twenty-ninth day he opens the ball, and throws it into the water, and from it the scarabaei come forth'.

The Greek writer, Plutarch also states:

'The Egyptians also honoured...the beetle, since they observed in them certain dim likenesses of the power of the gods.....The race of beetles has no female.....'

The Egyptian name for the scarab, which was perceived as another aspect of Ra was Khephri. The name comes from words meaning 'to come into existence' and 'stages of growth'. The sun deities were thought to have brought themselves into existence by masturbation, in common with the scarab's supposed lack of a female. Scarabs, as life-giving symbols were conferred on both the living and the dead. Combined with the image of the cat, the amulet became a symbol of supreme power.

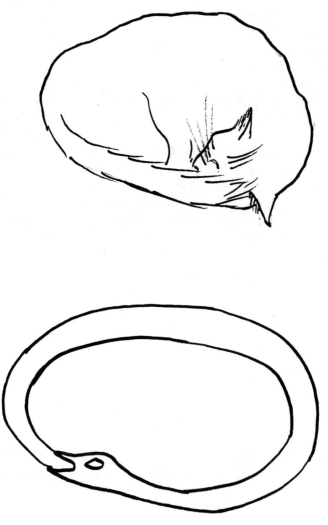

Sleeping cat and Ourobos

CHAPTER 3

THE CAT AND THE SERPENT

The serpent is a creature of great antiquity which is to be found in almost all mythologies worldwide. Even cultures which have no snakes, (such as the Eskimos and the Irish). still mention them in their legends

The serpent and the cat have a great deal in common, more than is immediately obvious. When they do not work in harmony together, they are bitter enemies.

Both love to bask in the sun. Both curl themselves into a circle, signifying eternity. Both symbolise the reconciliation of opposites. Both are considered royal emblems. Both are reputed to be healers. Both are guardians of sacred places. Both are oracular. Both signify rebirth: the snake by shedding it's skin and the cat with nine lives.

In Egyptian mythology, the snake was originally the Eye of the Creator which was later transformed into a cat. The snake in the form of the asp was like the cat, symbolic of the sun; it's darting tongue thought to resemble the penetrative solar rays. Both indicate carnal lust. Both have been considered as incarnations of evil. Both have been kept in households to control rodents. Both hiss and spit. Both have an unblinking gaze. The cat has been called a 'furry snake'.

Serpent mythology is one of the earliest beliefs and these primal serpents are generally bi-sexual. They existed before anything and inhabited the vast abyss of the primordial oceans which encircle the earth. This does not mean that the serpent is intrinsically evil. In many cases it is a benign creature, offering wisdom, prophecy and healing.

The serpent was called Leviathan by the Jews, the serpent of Midgard by the Norse and Tiamat by the Babylonians. The supreme goddess of Lower Egypt was called Ua-Zet (Uatchet, Buto, Uto or Uajyt). Whereas many cultures defeated or killed their serpents, it survived in Egypt: It is the uraeus, emblem of royalty on the forehead of Ra. The link continues: during the times of the Old and Middle Kingdoms (2686-1786 B.C.E.), daughters of noble families had the title of 'prophetess'. It was the goddesses Net and Hathor whose priestesses they became.

Because they are usually to be found in caves, crevices and under stones, Serpents were thought to inhabit the underworld and have knowledge of the kingdom of the dead. Demeter, the Greek mother Goddess of Corn and the Underworld has links with the cat and the snake.

The serpent as an agent of healing is found in close association with Asclepius, the god of healing in Greek myth. Asclepius, whose symbol is the snake, is the son of Apollo, whose attributes include prophecy, healing and light. The Greek word for snake is almost identical to the name Asclepius. (Apollo's sister Artemis invented the cat). Diagnoses and cures were based on a state of altered consciousness or dreams. Snake venom produces this state of being. The snake also symbolises renewal by the shedding of it's skin. Isis and Bastet are both connected with healing. Bastet herself was bitten by a scorpion and there are verses addressed to her, giving instructions for curing a cat of poison. (The Metternich Stele, Metropolitan Museum, New York). Scarabs have been found which are inscribed, 'Bastet, the nurse'. To this day some people believe that if the cat leaves a home, illness will be sure to take it's place. Isis is an incarnation of the Great Serpent.

The Celtic healer-god, Diancecht healed blindness by transplanting the eyes of a cat. Both cat and serpent have suffered cruelty in their association with healing. This association tells us that the cause of our illness may be within us - a lack of harmony and balance. Both cat and serpent are symbols of the unconscious and the hidden.

To this day, the medical profession uses the caduceus of Mercury: two serpents entwined round a wand, as their emblem. The two serpents symbolise the powers of the sun and moon which, when in harmony, lend their power to the operator which he/she directs with the wand. Spiritual healing depends upon the inner harmony of the healer to act as a channel.

The priests of Apollo destroyed the Delphic oracle, where a priestess, the Pythia, sat on a tripod stool giving prophecy. Around the stool's legs was coiled a Python. The site was originally known as Pytho. Herodotus referred to Bastet as 'Mistress of the Oracle'. Bastet is equated with Uajytt and she is therefore the Egyptian counterpart of the Delphic Oracle.

Taliesin says, *I have been a cat with spotted head upon a tripod*' - he may have been referring to himself as an oracle.

Irish legend tells of an oracular cat who reclined on a silver throne. In common with the Pythia, it would give a scathing reply to silly questions. A cat in Russia sat atop a golden pillar speaking to all who would listen. To the east, black cats were considered prophetic and Sinh, the Birmese cat was consulted in all spiritual matters.

Searching through myths and legends we find that serpents were systematically fought and vanquished by sun/sky divinities. The list is long:

> Ra fought with Zet/Apep/Apophis
> Enki/Marduk fought with Tiamat
> Zeus fought with Typhon
> Apollo fought with the Python
> Yahweh fought with Leviathan
> Thor fought with the Midgard serpent
> St. George fought with the Dragon
> St. Patrick expelled the snakes from Ireland.

At sunrise, Ra, in the form of a cat 'fought hard by the Persea tree'. The name 'Set' or 'Zet' means 'Queen'. The word 'Zet' also means serpent. It therefore follows that 'queen' and 'serpent' were synonymous and Set has probably changed sex in an attempt to obliterate earlier beliefs. (The same thing happened to Ashtoreth, the Mesopotamian goddess of love, fertility and war. In the Old Testament she is described as a male demon).

Set is identified with the Greek Typhon. The last of the chthonic children of the Earth, a being formed of coiled serpents from the thighs down. His arms were composed of snakes. At first the Typhon managed to overcome the invaders of Greece who escaped to Egypt in animal or bird form: Mercury as an ibis, Apollo as a crane and Artemis as a cat (who subsequently fled up to the moon). The ibis is sacred to Thoth (God of communication and wisdom), the crane to Ra-Osiris and the cat to Bastet.

In the story of the Fall of Man, the serpent takes centre stage and is later joined by a cat. To the ancient Hebrews, the Tree of Knowledge was understood to be not an apple tree, but a sycamore-fig or black mulberry (ficus sicomorus). Now this tree is sacred to Hathor. The fruit was eaten by her priestesses and known as the 'body and fluid' of the Goddess. It was this fruit that she offered to souls on their way to the Underworld.

Eve was the second wife of Adam. His first wife, Lilith, considered herself Adam's equal and spurned his advances. She left him and despite the entreaties of angels, refused to return. There is a Seferim legend in Spain which states that Lilith turned into a black cat called El Broosha. Lilith equates with Cat-Annis of East Anglia and, (according to Robert Graves in 'The White Goddess'), the goddess Cardea: all enemies of children. It is a reason why May blossom should not be brought into the house - Cardea may follow it. (May cats are unlucky and said to damage the health of children by sucking their breath). Lilith is now considered a demon in Cabbalistic tradition, synonymous with extreme carnality.

The tale as related in *Genesis* does not really make sense: why was the serpent (Hathor) inviting Eve into her service? Eve, as primeval woman was already her priestess. Should not the serpent have seduced Adam? Adam was easily enough persuaded by a woman, so why not by a goddess?

Enter the sky-divinity, Yahweh and the scene turns into the sky-sun god v. serpent battle which is so common in myth. Yahweh does, however, attempt to finish the relationship between woman and the serpent-goddess once and for all. It was the goddess Hathor who taught humanity how to reproduce themselves. His curse on Eve thenceforth, brings pain and sorrow to what must have formerly been regarded as a sacred rite: that of childbirth. Woman was forbidden to receive prophecy and wisdom and relay it to others: this is found in the later Paulian texts where women are charged to 'be silent in church' and 'obedient to their husbands'. 'Feminine intuition' is still viewed with disdain by some.

The account is also very unflattering to Adam: his first wife deserted him and the second persuaded him into a lifetime of toil and tribulation.

The cat is not mentioned in the Biblical version of 'The Fall'. However, the animal is alluded to by it's relationship with the serpent, Hathor and it's earlier association with Lilith. Later Christian art, depicting the cat as sly, lascivious and treacherous in common with the attitudes prevailing at the time, have ironically made the link which the Bible has omitted. The Old Testament does not link the serpent with the Devil, but the Apocrypha does, in the book of Wisdom ch2 v24. This was a rabbinic idea which influenced later Christian attitudes: when both the serpent and the cat were considered agents of the Devil.

In the Coptic gospel, *Pistis Sophia*, Jesus tells his mother how the world is surrounded by the ourobos, the cosmic serpent which holds it's tail in it's mouth. Within the body of this serpent are twelve halls of judgement. Each hall has it's particular officer who metes out justice. In the second hall is an officer who 'hath as his true face the face of a cat' and in the eleventh hall there are seven similar cat-faced officers.

Now the Copts were the early Egyptian Christians, and this account may have it's origins in the cult of Osiris as Lord of the Dead. Osiris often took cat-form.

The Mithraic god who equates with Saturn represents cosmic time. Zervan is shown as having the torso of a man, the head of a lion and is entwined with the cosmic serpent. Zervan had a counterpart among the Ophitic (serpent) sect of the Gnostics, called Ialdabaoth. Ialdabaoth was regarded as a creative force, is sometimes cat-headed and whose doctrines found their way into the beliefs of the Cathars and Albigensians. These 'heretics' were accused of worshipping Satan in the form of a black cat.

Far to the north, the Teutonic myth of the Midgard Serpent had a similar link. The Midgard Serpent was the offspring of Loki and a hag who was the 'Mother of Evil'. The Serpent had one aim in it's existence and that was to destroy creation. Odin knew that it's intention was to kill Thor. Thor threw the serpent over the walls of Asgard, the abode of the gods, whence it fell into the waters which encircle the earth.

Thor, accompanied by Loki, journeyed into the land of the Frost Giants who were ravaging the earth with a long winter. Upon entering the castle, the two were given feats of strength to prove themselves. One of the tests put to Thor was to lift a large cat. Thor put all his strength into the task, but only succeeded in lifting one paw from the earth.

Humiliated, Thor prepared to leave the following morning. The giant king asked if he was satisfied with his visit and Thor confessed his shame. The king admitted that the task given was impossible to do, for the cat was, in reality, the Midgard Serpent and when Thor lifted a paw, the giants were terrified that Thor should lift the whole animal and thus destroy the universe. This tale is similar to that told of Dermot and the Cat. The Celts also believed that if you trod on a cat's tail, a serpent would appear and sting you.

A Breton story tells of a green serpent who had once been a prince but who was bewitched into his present form by a white female cat.

An ancient Chinese legend tells of an Emperor who owned a beautiful cat. One day the Emperor was surprised to see his cat bathing in a pool which had collected water after three days of heavy rain. As he watched, the cat changed into a dragon, flew off and was never seen again.

The cat is on record as having eaten the rat which was bringing medicine to Buddha. Snakes also eat rodents and the viper, along with the cat failed to weep at Buddha's funeral. Both were barred.

The Mexican goddess of the earth is Coatlicue. She is the 'Serpent Lady', the mother from whom all creation came. She is life and death. All is in her. Her cult was closely linked with that of the jaguar.

The Chilean god of the lakes and seas was Ngurvilu. He caught his victims in the form of a cat and killed them as a serpent.

Nearer to our own time, information extracted as confessions at the witch trials during the seventeenth century, compares the Devil's semen to snake venom and the witches themselves were called Valkyries or furies. The demons had snake form, symbolic of the Earth mother in her destructive aspect. The Devil and witches had strong association with the cat.

There are some beliefs concerning snakes and cats which are identical:

A live adder is still believed in some areas to presage ill-luck and to find one alive on the doorstep, a sure sign of a death. It is also believed that a snake cannot die before sunset, an echo of the time when the snake was a form of the sun and both 'died' when the sun disappeared below the horizon.

To kill the first snake you saw during the springtime was 'lucky' (not for the snake though). If we consider the month of May as springtime, May cats were also drowned as they were 'useless mousers' and brought live snakes into the house.

The dried skin of a snake protects the house from fire and draws good luck. Worn around the knee, relieves rheumatism and round the head, a headache. Women in protracted labour were advised to bind a snake-skin around themselves to ease and speed the birth. Cat skins were also used medicinally.

Teutonic customs, which are still found in Lithuania and Latvia were to keep a snake in the house to destroy rodents. It was considered as a minor house-spirit. The Romans believed that a (live) cat in the house had the same effect.

48

CHAPTER 4

CHILD OF THE MOON

Cats have long been associated with the moon. If they bask all day in the heat of the sun, or drowse by the fire, it is in keeping with the dual aspect of their natures that they also enjoy hunting and mating by the light of the moon at night.

The cat's eyes are said to be representations of the lunar orb. Egyptians believed that Ra entrusted the cat to carry the glow of the sun throughout the night as a promise of his return the following morning. The moon rules the three phases of our lives, youth, maturity and old age. However, it is with the life-cycle of women that the moon is particularly associated, which can be traced in most mythologies in the person of the moon goddess. She is the personification of the feminine part of our psyches.

The feminine is that part of us which controls creativity, intuition, imagination, instinct, the arts, writing, music and dance, design, mediumship and clairvoyance. The feminine does not judge, it accepts, it does not label. The feminine takes masculine power and transforms it into a new creation that is more than the sum of the parts. The birth of a child is such an event. The masculine within us (the sun) controls logic, reason. judgement, language, science. It builds, controls, labels, directs and organises. The masculine gives law, structure and substance to our lives, it examines cause and effect. Lacking the masculine, we would do nothing, go nowhere and never progress.

Without the feminine, our lives would be regimented, drab and cheerless, lacking in warmth, harmony and colour. These are extreme examples but should serve to illustrate the difference. Both are equal in merit and worth.

Many men have the feminine strongly developed in their psyches: men who are drawn to the arts: painters, writers . (Ernest Hemingway, when writing 'A Farewell to Arms' had thirty-four cats living in his Cuban home) and designers. This is not to say that they are effeminate. (Nor does this imply that these gentlemen all like cats - or women. The painter Cezanne called all women 'damned cats!'). Feminine attributes can function through a masculine outlook as masculine qualities may through a feminine outlook, which gives us the rich diversity of life.

As cats are traditionally associated with women, it is this relationship which will be examined, but please bear in mind that much of what is written applies equally to those gentlemen in whom the creative side of their personality is well developed.

There is a fascinating painting by the artist Leonora Carrington called 'Tuesday'. It shows women with cats, both Siamese and tabbies. One woman has a second, feline, head growing from her shoulders. The artist may be pointing to the close connection of the cat and the feminine. Whatever the artist intended, the work affords plenty of food for the imagination.

The feminine world is, like the cat, unfathomable, enigmatic and mysterious. It covers the gamut of emotions from languid, beguiling disdain to deep rage and the blind jealousy of the betrayed. The goddess Venus is at once a warm, affectionate little kitten and a savage, spiteful cat armed with tooth and claw. There is nothing quite so painful to the soul as love denied, unrequited or rejected. Nothing evokes such hatred towards an erstwhile amour than betrayal. 'Hell hath no fury' indeed.

Venus is a favourite subject for artists - look carefully and you will usually see the goddess of love accompanied by a small animal: a cat or rabbit. The rabbit shares the a similar sexual reputation to the cat. The Romans, credited with it's introduction to Britain considered it's flesh a delicacy. (In later years, cat carcasses, skinned, were passed off as rabbits in markets. Both look alike when undressed). The rabbit is also an animal sacred to the Moon. Chinese astrology equates the cat with the Sign of the Rabbit, not as would be supposed, with the Sign of the Tiger.

The moon goddesses were triple divinities, an aspect representing each phase of the lunar cycle: Let us see how the cat relates to them:

The new and waxing moon represents creative potential. The goddess of this phase is called the Maiden. An old saying was, 'What's begun at the new is completed at the full'. Useful to remember if you wish to plant seeds by the moon or begin and complete a project. Diana and Artemis, virgin-huntresses rule the waxing moon: with arrows (moonbeams) fired from silver (lunar) bows, these shafts pierce the darkness of night (ignorance) and penetrate our subconscious, bringing enlightenment, helping us to mature. They also hunt the souls of men, for the male energy to initiate into life. Their representative the cat also hunts by night, it's prey the mouse is symbolic of the soul in many cultures. Diana is depicted as riding on a black cat in engravings of the witch trials and Artemis is said to have fled to the moon in the shape of a cat.

The following legend illustrates the 'predatory' aspect of the virgin goddess, Diana, in her need to create. It was given to an American folklorist, Charles Godfrey Leland by an Italian witch during the last century.

> *'Before all things were made, there existed only Diana. She existed in the darkness and was the potential source of all things. She divided herself into male and female.. Her light (male) aspect she called Lucifer (Light Bearer). She looked on him and desired him.*
>
> *Lucifer repulsed her advances although she visited him each night. One day, she noticed that Lucifer had a fairy cat which slept on his bed. Diana summoned the cat and persuaded it to change shapes with her (even a goddess cannot force a cat). From the union was born a daughter, Aradia, who taught magic and wisdom to humanity in the name of Diana'.*

Diana is the witch-goddess, mentioned in the *Canon Episcopi*, the Church's original pronouncement on witchcraft. Many illustrations show Diana with a cat at her feet or flying to the Sabbat or the Wild Hunt astride a cat. The Moon rules fertility, the mind and water: these three topics were constantly mentioned during the witch trials.

It is important to understand why virgin goddesses are also mothers. The problem arises in the original use and subsequent distortion, of the word, virgin.

The original meaning was of a woman who was unwed, had experienced sexual relations with a man (or god), but remained independent and 'her own woman'. She did not 'belong' to him, neither was she bound by emotional constraint. The modern definition is a woman who has not experienced sexual relations at all.

The Virgin Mary was betrothed to Joseph but was, in Biblical terms, unmarried. It was later thought to be an immodest situation for the mother of the Messiah and the meaning was subtly altered.

It is interesting that virgin-goddesses are also patronesses of women in childbirth - they aid the final act of bringing their potential into being. The full moon, now rounded as in an advanced pregnancy, represents the mother. The full moon is the lovers' moon when, as an Egyptian papyrus states, 'couplings and conceptions abound'. The female creative principle is brought to maturity. She is completion and fulfilment.

The mother-goddesses are Isis/Bastet/Mut, Demeter/Ceres, Dana/Erin, and Cerridwen. The list is by no means complete. All mother goddesses give life and continue to nourish life, both on a physical and mental/spiritual level.

On the physical plane, she rules motherhood, children, fertility, healing and harvest. The cat enjoys her motherhood and woe betide any who attempt to interfere with her. Plutarch maintained that a cat's reproductive cycle was as follows: the queen would produce one kitten in the first litter, then two in the second until she reached her seventh, then bearing seven kittens. After this her reproductive life was finished. The number seven is a number of completion, a boundary has been reached after which a new phase begins. The total number of kittens born is twenty-eight, the number of days in a lunar month. Plutarch was wrong in his assessment; the female cat can become a mother three or four times during the year and come into heat every three weeks, especially during the Spring. She can produce between three and five kittens at each birth. An interesting idea, all the same.

When the moon was thought to be a masculine deity, women believed the light from the full moon would cause pregnancy. Khonsu, the son of Mut and god of the moon was said to make women fruitful and aid the growth of seed in the womb.

Amulets of a cat and kittens were exchanged by newly-married Egyptian couples. The amulet was enamelled in either blue or green and showed a mother-cat with kittens: the number of kittens represented the corresponding number of children the couple wished to have. The colours blue and green belong to Venus who also equates to Bastet as goddess of sexual pleasure and fulfilment.

In central Europe, a cat would be brought into the bedroom of the newly-married couple and rocked in the cradle. A Russian tradition is to put a cat into a baby's cradle to protect the child from evil spirits. An east Anglian custom was to make a little cape out of ferret, stoat or cat fur and pad it with sheep's wool. Pubic hair from a boy was put into one side and that from a girl was put into the other side. A fertility symbol, made from the fur of prolific animals.

When Christianity became the official religion of the Roman Empire, the cult of the mother continued with Mary, the mother of the sun child, Christ. Legend tells that when he was born, a cat gave birth to kittens beneath the manger at the same time. Little is told of Christ's mother in the Bible but the doctrine which has subsequently grown around her reflects the continuing religious beliefs from earlier cults of the Great Mother. Mary inherited the title, 'Stella Maris', Star of the Sea from Isis. The moon rules the seas.

On another level, the mother represents the fruit of the mind and spirit: she is present when a task is completed which has demanded a lot of yourself. The zodiacal sign of Cancer relates to the mother. The fertilising strength of the male sun is found not in the sun's own (male) sign of Leo, but in Cancer. The summer solstice marks the sun at his greatest strength - and occurs when it enters the sign of the Waters of Life. When Isis searched for the dismembered parts of Osiris' body, she found all but his phallus: this had been eaten (absorbed) by a crab (Cancer) in the Waters of Life (the Nile).

The waning moon, or when the grows smaller and approaches the 'dark of the moon' represents the withdrawal of fertility from body into the subconscious. The mother is aged, her young have left her to continue the cycle. She mourns their loss as she would a dead child. In mythology this phase is told in the legends of dying sons and daughters abducted into the Underworld. The mother becomes the crone. The word crone does not imply an evil old woman: far from it; the word may have some connection with 'chronos', time. It is this phase which stores up in itself wisdom and knowledge. The wisdom and knowledge which is only gained from experience and suffering. Those who wish to have these attributes pay a great price to obtain them: age. There is no going back. She is mistress of the hidden and the unseen.

Many post-menopausal women are able to transform their innate creativity. They 'magically' influence the lives of others with their wisdom and understanding. The arts,

counselling and social work all benefit. Death is the final barrier before enlightenment. Goddesses who represent this aspect of our lives are Hecate, Demeter and Isis. Hecate is thought to be Thracian in origin and is certainly older than the Olympians. She may have originally been closely associated with the cat, although nowadays it is usually the howling dog. (Dogs do bay at the moon, as do their ancestors, the wolf. However, as Hecate is the mistress of ghosts and spirits, which dogs dislike intensely, perhaps the original animal was not a dog, but a cat?) The following legend sheds light on Hecate's feline past:

The goddess Hera was furious that her husband Zeus had fathered a child on yet another woman. This time he had masqueraded as the husband of Alcmene and Hercules was the result of that union. Hera determined that the child should not be born, and placed magical guardians at Alcmene's door to force her into nine days' labour.

Galinthias, a faithful servant girl of Alcmene, tricked the guards into breaking the spell and assisted at the birth. As a punishment, Hera changed Galinthias into a cat and banished her to the underworld where she became a priestess of Hecate. Galinthias was, moreover, condemned to bear her young through her mouth (it was popularly believed that cats bore their young this way because this was how they carried them).

Another explanation is because she told lies about the birth to Hera. (Some accounts state that Galinthias was turned into a lizard or a weasel: in the latter case, there may be some justification, as the Greek word for weasel is 'gale').

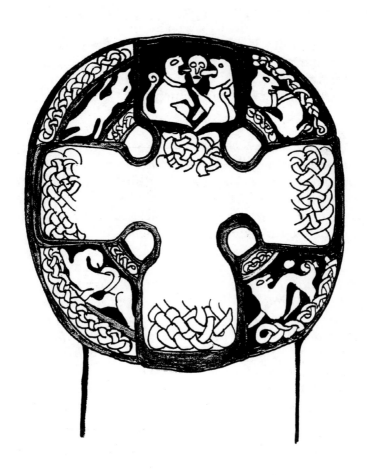

Detail of Kirk Braddon Cross

There is a further link: as mistress of secret knowledge, Hecate is said to haunt cross-roads. Offerings were left for her at such places and criminals hanged there. A cat tied to a place where five ways met then released was said to lead to treasure. Shakespeare mentions Hecate in '*Macbeth*' and so does his contemporary, Thomas Middleton, in '*The Witch*'.

Both Isis and Demeter know grief and loss. Isis grieves over the dead body of her husband/brother Osiris, and Demeter walks the earth seeking her abducted daughter, Persephone. As these two goddesses withdrew from the world, the earth became barren. Both goddesses had, in common with Hecate, rulership over the Underworld. In Greek myth, the dead were called 'Demeter's People'. The legends of Demeter and Isis formed the basis of mystery cults which dominated the ancient world. They were of great importance because they offered the concept of life after death or reincarnation. The cult of Isis was brought to Britain by the Romans. There was a Thames-side temple to her in London and an altar has been found to her in Chester. The upper Thames is still called the Isis.

It was in the worship of these goddesses that the chthonian aspect of religion reached it's zenith.

There is an interesting cross to be seen inside the Church at Old Kirk Braddan, on the Isle of Man. The cross is about four feet four inches in height and three feet two inches across the widest part. What is of particular interest is the design: At the top of the upright arm is a motif showing a human face between two cat or lion-like animals. Between the arms of the cross are four animals. Three look very much like cats and the fourth could be a mouse or shrew. They are shown in the style of Celtic animals as drawn in the illuminated manuscripts. What the cross actually signifies is open to interpretation. It has been suggested that the central head and two cats represents Daniel in the Lions' Den. However, Plutarch states that, 'the human countenance between two cat-like figures upon a stone, infers that the changes of the moon's phases are regulated by wisdom and understanding'.

In the Chavin culture of Peru (c 1200B.C.E) similar motifs are widespread. (Peru was the religious centre of the cat-god cult). They are also found in India.

According to the Greek poet, Demetrius Phalarius, The three cats growing increasingly plump signify the changing phase of the moon. The last figure, if a mouse or a shrew-mouse fits in well: the shrew-mouse (or mygale) is symbolic of the incarnation of Horus, Isis' son. When Set tore out Horus' left eye, it was returned to him by wise Thoth as the full moon. The cross, although outwardly Christian, may tell of the passage of time and the love of the Queen of Heaven for her Son which passes all boundaries.

Discussion of the Triple-Goddess would be incomplete without reference to the number nine. Time and time again, the number three and nine occur in folklore, myth and legend. Ancient charms and prayers for healing call upon the Trinity and this may cause some confusion as the concept of the Trinity was originally female, but later came to refer to the Christian Trinity. In many instances, it is not certain which Trinity is meant: it must surely, therefore depend on personal belief.

The number nine is connected with both cats and the moon.

The number sacred to the goddess is three. Therefore the number sacred to the triple goddess is nine

The fateful hour of Christ's death was the ninth: from that time the Virgin Mary became the sorrowing mother.

There are nine months required to bring a pregnancy to full term.

Odin gave Freya power over nine worlds.

The river Styx encircles the underworld in nine concentric circles.

The Egyptian pantheon consisted of three groups of nine deities.

A cat has nine lives.

A witch can take cat-form nine times.

An expression frequently used with ancient myth and legend is 'a year and a day'. This period of time is based on the lunar year of thirteen months. Each lunar month consists of twenty-eight days. $13 \times 28 = 364$. The extra day is added on to make up the equivalent of the solar year, 365 days. Some cultures, e.g. the Chinese and the Jewish calendars still reckon time by the lunar year.

CHAPTER 5

THE CAT OF EARTH AND STONE

The Earth is our home. All we have, all we do and all we are depends upon the Earth. Our food comes from the fields and is stored in barns and granaries. We make shelters and call them homes. The materials for these come from the Earth, be it the stone castle, baronial manor or wattle-and-daub cottage. All come from the Earth. Protection, then from fire, flood, wind or pestilence was essential to our forebears who had not the benefit of supermarket, freezer or insurance policy to help out when things went wrong. In this chapter we will look at the way the cat has guarded field and barn, home and hearth in the past.

Field and Barn

The fertility of the Earth was a matter of life and death to our ancestors. They were entirely dependent upon the weather, state of the soil, fertility of the seed - and the beneficence of their gods. We are still dependent on the good Earth for our food: all life depends on it. Even today, with an efficient transport system to convey food to distant lands, an agrichemical industry to wrench the last ounce of fertility from our soils and long-range weather forecasting we are still at the mercy of Nature.

Fertility of the soil was passed from the gods into the body of the reigning monarch. The king had to be above reproach in his dealings with the gods, the land and the people: the blame for a failed harvest was laid at the king's door and he could pay for it with his life. During the reign of the usurper, Cairbre Caitcheann in Ireland, only one grain grew on each stalk of corn, one acorn on each oak, rivers became empty of fish and the cattle died. Cairbre had the ears of a cat.

Early people envisaged the life of their crops in the form of an animal which they called the 'corn spirit'. The particular animal chosen as representative varied with location and belief. The horse, hare, cock, wolf, goat, sow or - cat.

The cat as a corn spirit? The idea comes from antiquity: the cat is a fertile animal and is the enemy of the destroyers of grain, mice and rats.

Deities who were linked with the growth of vegetation were invariably also rulers of the underworld or deities of death and/or destruction. Among these are Mars, Saturn, Demeter/Ceres, Venus/Aphrodite and Osiris. There are many others. The agricultural attributes of both Mars and Saturn are often overshadowed by their other aspects as rulers of war and limitation respectively. The fire of Mars symbolises growth as well as war. The Earthy Saturn rules the stirring of the seed at the birth of the sun in Capricorn. Mars is the lover of Cat-Venus and Saturn's animal is the cat.

Other deities take their places in an almost universal legend of a wife/mother who seeks for her lost/dead husband or child only to find him/her in the Underworld. Their release is possible but only partial: a period of time in the Underworld is demanded by it's ruler.

The legend of Demeter seeking her lost daughter Persephone, who has been abducted by Hades is the prototype of myths which explain seasonal change. Modern versions of the myth say that Persephone spent the winter months with Hades. This is wrong. She spent that time of the year with him when the ground was non-productive. In southern Mediterranean lands this is during hot summer months when the earth is parched and barren. Grain is sown during the autumn and harvested during the early summer. It is a case of applying climatic conditions of north-west Europe to a southern myth which is misleading. The time is better understood to mean the barren months of the year (irrespective of season), which gives flexibility for geographical location. Persephone is the growing corn and as Demeter, she is the ripe corn ready for harvesting.

When Persephone left the Underworld, she ate seven seeds of the pomegranate. The pomegranate is the fruit which symbolises both fertility and death (and was the emblem of the hapless Catherine of Aragon who only bore Henry VIII one living child of many still-born). It was accepted that to partake of food and drink in the Underworld meant that one would never leave it. This is reminiscent of Hathor offering nourishment to the dead from her sycamore-fig tree, the Tree of Life.

The number seven is also important here as a number of completion. Seven is always found as a complete quantity (seven days in a week, colours in the rainbow) and points to the end of a cycle. Demeter's emblems are an ear of wheat and the poppy. The poppy is a narcotic flower of rest and death. As the corn-mother, Demeter has association with the cat who protects the grain.

Hades rules the Underworld and it's wealth. His other name, Pluto, means riches, although this may refer to minerals it is more likely to mean the growing seed. The name of Hades' Roman equivalent, Dis Pater also means 'wealth'.

The Egyptian deity of vegetation and the Underworld are one and the same, Osiris. Osiris was annually murdered by his brother Set. His sister/wife, Isis managed to conceive from Osiris' partially-revived body after which he became ruler of the underworld. In this role he equates with Hades in his responsibility for the 'wealth' of the Underworld, i.e. the growing seed. While Osiris remains in the Underworld, his son Horus is born of Isis. Horus and Osiris equate with Persephone (growing corn) and Demeter (ripe corn). Once again, we find the number seven in the name of Set, from which is the French word for seven, 'sept'. Saturn is the planetary vehicle of Set, which lends it's name to the seventh day of the week. As an early deity of sown seed, and the use of his temple as the state treasury, Saturn also has much in common with Hades.

During the festivities of harvest, Osiris was often depicted as a cat or with a cat. In the temple of Isis at Philae, the body of the murdered Osiris is shown with corn sprouting from it. A priest sprays it with water. In Cairo Museum a statuette shows Osiris sitting between Nefertem and Horus. At their feet is a female cat.

The Celtic goddess Cerridwen brought grain to Britain. After she had sown it, she gave birth to a cat, Cath Palug.

Venus is not often thought of as goddess of growth, but she is responsible for gardens, vineyards and flowers. A small-scale harvest but just as vital as the corn-fields. Venus has been linked with Greek Aphrodite and the Canaanite Innana. Aphrodite has a dark side to her nature and in her aspect as Aphrodite Pasiphaessa, she is Queen of the Underworld. Aphrodite quarrelled with Persephone over her lover, Adonis and it was decided that Adonis should spend one third of his time in the Underworld.

Innana is the goddess of Earth and moon. Later tradition linked her with Annis and the Cailleach Bheur, both of whom are connected with cats and are dangerous to children.

Paintings of Venus as goddess of love frequently depict her with a cat.

Above the grainfields, the sun's rays could either ripen or scorch the harvest. The Egyptians relied on Ra, as the Great Cat to ripen their corn, but through intermediaries through whom the heat is controlled, Isis the corn mother or her daughter Bastet, the mild heat of the sun. Isis-Bastet are cat goddesses.

All over Europe, rituals were enacted celebrating the cat-spirit of the corn. Children were warned by their parents not to play in the fields of growing corn. If they trampled it the phantom cat of the fields would devour them (this is similar to the threat made to children concerning Cat Annis of eastern England). If a reaper should cut himself with a scythe, he should immediately seek a cat to lick the wound, lest the harvest be lost.

In the Dauphine region of France, a cat was bound in swaddling bands and decorated with ribbons and flowers at the beginning of reaping. Named the 'cat of the ball-skin'. The last sheaf gathered in French harvesting was called the Cat's Tail. The man who cut it put it on his shoulder, took a partner and together they would chase all the other workers to bring good luck to field and bakery.

The Silesian reaper who cut the last stand was called a 'Tom-Cat' and another reaper was the 'She-Cat'. Both were decorated with rye stalks and plaited tails after which, they chased everyone in sight.

Germany has similar traditions: The crop itself is known as 'The cat' and described as lean or fat according to the prospects. He who cut the last sheaf was called 'Catcher of the Corn-Cat' and presented with a bouquet or a small fir-tree, decorated with ribbons. In Hildersheim, a cat was secured in a basket which was pulled to the top of a fir-tree. The fir-tree or pine is an ancient symbol of fertility and rebirth and is thus associated with the Earth/Corn/Mother Goddesses. The term 'fir' and 'pine' here include any member of the coniferous family of trees. Celebrations of the Thesmophoria included food and pine branches placed in caves. A year later they were removed and displayed on the altars of Demeter. Worshippers then buried them in furrows along with the seed corn for the following season. The festival of the Goddess Cybele involved the ritual felling of a pine which was decorated with the blood of her son/lover Attis. This is another variant of the cutting of the corn, burial and regrowth.

Osiris was buried in a hollowed-out pine log which was burnt the following year, the ashes being scattered on the earth and when Set scattered the body of Osiris on the land, it was symbolic of scattering the grain. Some years ago, an Egyptian bronze came up for sale at Sotheby's. It showed a winged man standing on a crocodile (Set), symbols of Osiris and Bastet were engraved upon it. In place of the missing genitalia was a cat's head.

The ancient Peruvian god of Agriculture is shown as a wizened man with whiskers and long teeth. This is Ai-Apaec who also rules fertility, hunting and healing.

When goodness is taken from the earth, it must be returned in order to secure another harvest. The corn-spirit had to be returned to the fields. The sacrificial cat (or whatever animal was perceived as embodying the spirit), met it's end in the Midsummer fires and the ashes strewn on the fields to bring an abundant harvest. By so doing, the god was sacrificed to himself. Midsummer was propitious as after this time the sun lost strength. The unfortunate victim was intended to add extra energy.

Far to the east, Chinese reapers held a celebration to their harvest deity, Li-Shou. Li-Shou in the body of a cat, protected the gathered grain. Sacrifices were made to cats who devoured rats and mice which would otherwise the ruin the precious harvest. A refreshing change from the European custom of murdering the cats which would have protected theirs.

While honest folk worked hard to produce healthy crops of grain and vegetables, others did their best to damage the harvest. Below is an example of a spell using the fertile aspect of the cat used negatively, to destroy by calling on the aid of Satan:

> 'Fill the skin of a cat with vegetable matter. Put in a well or spring for three days. Dry and grind to a powder. Scatter from a high place on a windy day as a sacrifice to Satan who will oblige by destroying crops'.

Without the warmth and light of the sun, the crops would not grow nor the corn ripen.

Home and Hearth

The spirit of a cat was thought to protect the building. In both Scandinavia and Britain, remains of cats have been found bricked up in walls or under floors. Some were found by construction workers in the Tower of London whilst excavating a ground-floor room. Less than thirty years ago, the mummified bodies of a cat and her kittens were discovered plastered in the wall of a cottage at Cricksea. They are now in a museum. Cat skeletons have been found under the floor of a Roman house at Colchester.

The Romans settled at Caerleon in Gwent where they built a considerable town and the amphitheatre can still be seen. One of their legacies was the use of protective tiles, fixed at the gable ends of buildings to avert evil. These tiles, known as *antefixa*, are found elsewhere in Britain, but those from Caerleon are of particular interest. The design on the *antefixae* are of human heads, a few of which have the ears of a cat.

Dr. Anne Ross mentions these in *'Pagan Celtic Britain'*. Caerleon is in the ancient land of Siluria and the Silurians were thought to have venerated the cat. These tiles may be the head of a local (as yet unknown) deity or they may refer to such Celtic legends as Cath Palug. The faces are very feline and the pine cones and branches (?) around the heads suggest a link with the cat's fertility aspect. A harvest custom was to hang a cat in a basket from pine trees during the harvest. I have included a sketch of them overleaf for readers to judge for themselves.

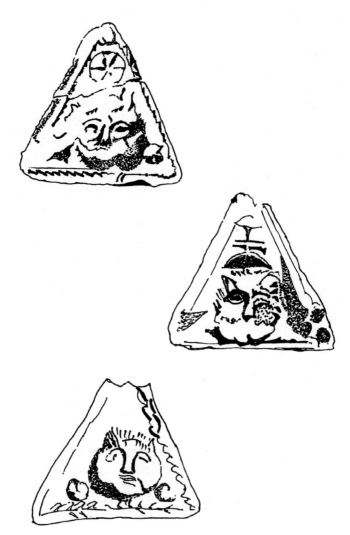

Sketches of 'Cat-Faced' Antefixa, Caerleon, Gwent

The Hearth

The hearth has been thought to be a sacred place for thousands of years. From being the fire round which early man crept for warmth and protection from wild beasts and evil spirits, to the heart of the home where the family still gather. The cat was also supposed to be able to offer protection against fire. A situation of 'fighting fire with fire'

In Europe, tri-coloured cats were thought to be particularly good for this purpose The Roman Goddess of the Hearth was Vesta. She guarded the fires of not only the households but the State itself as well. When the cat became a household pet it quickly rose to be a 'genius loci', the presiding spirit of the home. Perhaps the cat arrived in Rome too late for the Goddess to claim it as her own, for the cat who dreams before the fire is surely her animal.

The cat which originally was the fire, protects against fire and has suffered in the fire. In an apocryphal gospel, Jesus says, 'He that is near to Me is near the fire' He at once offers warmth and comfort at the same time danger and destruction. The cat which was born under His manger and which has suffered dreadfully, will understand those words.

The Cat and the Stone

When notable souls have passed back into the Earth at death, it has been the practice through the ages to use the very bones of the earth, stones to commemorate them. Statues of stone and marble were later superseded by bronze, but all these materials have come from the Earth herself.

It is not only the worthies who are remembered this way: some stones are reminders what can happen when we play with the powers of the unknown and somehow offend them. There are many stories of circles and standing stones which are said to come alive at certain critical times of the year, mainly at Beltane or Mid-summer, when the Earth energies are strong.

The Rollright stones of Oxfordshire are the petrified forms of a Danish king and his men who sought to invade England. They asked advice of a witch who managed to turn them into stone.

There are a few standing stones, dolmens or natural outcrops which attest to the deeds of witches who took cat form:

Scotland has several lone standing stones known as 'cat stanes'.

At Waternish, there is a stone known as the 'Cat's Cairn'. The cairn marks the spot where a boy accidentally came upon three women from the village in the process of turning themselves into cats. They made him promise to tell nobody, but eventually his mother managed to get the story from him. On top of the cairn is a long stone which is the spot where the boy was clawed to death for breaking his word.

From Japan comes the story of the witch who lived near the posting station on the Tokaido road. She was turned to stone because, in cat-form she frightened women on their way to the temple. The stone is still to be seen as a warning.

In France there is a dolmen near Sabarer, known as Prat des Gats (Field of Cats). It is reputed to be the home of a witch called Matebe. The name is similar to the French word for tomcat which is 'matou'. This dolmen has a similarity to the cave of Cat-Annis in the Leicestershire hills and may have a similar mythology.

Some natural stone outcrops are monuments to the witch-cats: Eagle's Crag near Burnley, Lancs. is the site of a witch's grave. She was Lady Sybil, wife of Sir William Towneley. Sir William married her, knowing that she was versed in magic. He made her promise to give it up once they were married, but she broke her word. She lost her hand while in the shape of a cat, and later died of the wound. She haunts the crag at Samhain (Hallowe'en).

Near Maidstone in Kent is a large block of sandstone resting upon three other stones. This is called Kit's Coty House.

Breaking a promise leads to an unstable situation, it damages the foundations of the personality. It becomes unreliable. To be turned into stone is a lesson in kind for others not to make the same mistake.

One monument to a cat which is well known to all is the milestone on Highgate Hill. On it sits Dick Whittington's cat in bronze. If the 'cat' was indeed a ship, as some theories suggest, somehow the monument would lose it's charm.

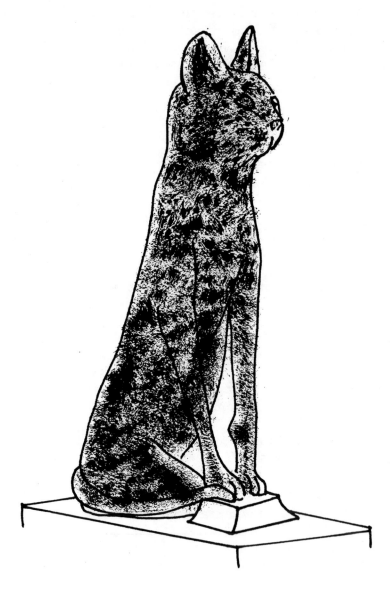

Cat reliquary of bronze with base. Abusir c500 B.C.E.
(British Museum)

CHAPTER 6

THE CAT AND THE UNDERWORLD

It is an inescapable fact of life that death comes to all: be we rich or poor, king or peasant, good or bad, young or old. Death eventually claims us. Birth and death were mysteries to early man and our attitudes to both have changed very little in recorded history. Man has always secretly believed that he should be immortal, like his gods. After all, the snake and crab were thought to renew themselves, why not us? Death is variously seen as a great mistake, a punishment or even the result of a Divine instruction which has been irretrievably lost or misunderstood.

Attitudes towards the deceased range from sorrow, love and awe to fear and even horror. The dead are never disregarded. (Even a regime which has no religion is respectful to the dead). Resting places for the body range from the simple Neolithic grave to caves, megaliths, pyramids and modern mausoleums. The soul journeys to another place, the location of which varies according to culture.

One place is the western horizon: this may be the ocean (Celtic and Greek) or desert (Egyptian). This is the place of the setting or 'dying' sun. Above the sky is another place: the Christian Heaven is situated here as is the boat of Ra. The third location is below the earth: the Greek and Roman Underworld, Christian Hell and the Osirian Ament.

The Eskimo people have a legend in which an elderly woman states that she would willingly give up dying even if there was no sunlight. Her companion thought for a while and decided that it were better to have both, for eternal life without the sunlight would be intolerable. A valid point, but some perceptions of the Underworld were no different: the Romans considered it to be a dimly-lit, shadow filled place where discarnate souls wandered aimlessly through eternity. No idea of punishment here, all shared this existence. To reach this land a river had to be crossed which erased all memory of the former life. The Greek Underworld was believed to be reached beyond the waters that encircled the earth. A gloomy wasteland ruled by Hades. When sailors discovered that lands to the west were pleasant, the Underworld was relocated beneath the earth. The wicked remained in Tartarus, a dreadful place while heroes and other worthies crossed the river Lethe and remained in the Elysian Fields.

The legends of Persephone-Demeter and Osiris-Isis both illustrate the necessary descent into the Underworld in order to release new life and growth. Underworld deities such as Pluto, Hades and Osiris are not gods of death or the personification of death. They have charge over the period of rest before regrowth or rebirth. The names Pluto and Hades mean 'wealth of the earth'. Precious metals and gemstones are not indicated here, but something more valuable - seed which is the gift of life.

In Early Egypt, the afterlife was for the Pharaoh only, with the later addition of the aristocracy. The Pyramid Texts at Saqqara dating from c2000B.C.E., give details for prayers, spells and rituals for use of the Pharaoh in the afterlife. Eternity was spent in the boat of Ra in the heavens, where all was light, even in the journey through the Fields of Aalu at night. Ra then became the Great Cat to fight for the sunrise.

With the rise of the cult of Osiris, the Underworld was known as Ament; the entrance was a subterranean opening just beneath the western horizon. In this case it was the desert not the ocean. The Egyptian Underworld was dark and airless.

Admittance to eternal life was by complicated burial rites, a hazardous journey (for which guidebooks were provided) followed by judgement. If favourable, the soul became Osiris and his name is thereafter placed before that of the deceased. Osiris may have been a king who was later deified. He controlled vegetation and the inundation of the Nile. He was god of the moon and the Underworld. All these are concerned with the passage of time and continuation of the cycle. As god of the Underworld, he like Pluto/Hades is responsible for the seed which has been planted in the earth. Plutarch gives a fuller account of the legend of Osiris than do Egyptian texts.

The Legend of Osiris

In the beginning, Osiris was principally concerned with vegetation and corn. He taught people the elements of agriculture, the use of grain for bread and grapes for wine. His jealous brother Set tricked him into entering a coffin, closed the lid and cast the coffin into the Nile. Isis sought her husband, tracing the coffin to Byblos where it had become encased in the trunk of a sycamore (some say tamarisk) tree.

Isis rescued her husband's body and hovered above it in the form of a sparrow-hawk, fanning breath into it. She managed to revive him enough to become pregnant with the future Horus.

Set thereupon took the body and hacked it into pieces, distributing them all over the land. Isis patiently sought each piece, finding all except the genitalia which had been eaten by a Nile crab or crocodile.

Isis embalmed the body and Osiris became the living god of the Underworld. The lack of genitalia precluded him from returning to earth - he was no longer fertile. Thus he remained in the Underworld where fertility is 'at rest'. Osiris is depicted as a mummified man crowned with the white crown of Upper Egypt. His crossed arms hold the flail (cat o' nine tails) and hook of royalty. One of his symbols is the djed, the tree-trunk, it represents his spine and stability. Another is the Bennu bird or Phoenix, symbolising rebirth.

The Egyptian account of this legend omits the coffin and discovery at Byblos, which is similar to Demeter seeking her daughter in a foreign land. The loss of the genitalia is also omitted. Plutarch was a priest of Apollo and may have added these events himself to fit in with the Demeter story.

Bastet, the daughter of Osiris had considerable influence in the Underworld. A cat was believed to oversee or take part in the funeral rites. A funerary papyrus shows a cat sitting upright, with a scarab beetle above it and an utchat below.

This is known as the 'Cat of Lapis Lazuli', the scarab and utchat indicate not Ra, but protection in the afterlife. The deity is Bastet or Osiris. The Egyptians believed that the 'ka' or personality could exist independently of the body and soul (ba). Each representation of deity, whether picture or statue, was imbued with this independent 'double' which acted as an aura.

Other protective tokens have been found, ivory wands with cats engraved upon them or cats' heads carved in the ends. The deities invoked are often those who destroy venomous snakes which are also believed to inhabit the Underworld.

A token has been discovered engraved with the words, 'May Bastet revivify the deceased among the glorified.'

A funerary text shows the passage of the soul of a woman from the temple of Amun-Ra. As a singer, she is sponsored by Bastet and presented to Osiris. At Bastet's feet is an ankh, held in the jaws of Ammut, the devourer of souls who have been found wanting in the scales of justice. Above the scene is a serpent and the words of Osiris, 'the justified one'.

The test of worthiness for continued life is for the heart to be weighed against the feather of Ma'at in the scales of justice. Truth and honest confession were vital. Ma'at has been called the 'Eye of Ra/Horus/Osiris' and as such is his representative. Some figurines and statues of Bastet show the hairs in her ears curled like the feather of Ma'at. Ma'at is the daughter of Ra and wife of Thoth, god of communication and writing. Thoth equates with Mercury/Hermes, who guides the dead to the Underworld. His caduceus, carrying the power of the sun and moon as two serpents are also the eyes of the cat and Osiris. From the papyrus of Ani in the Book of the Dead, the soul declares:

> *'Hail Bast, coming forth from the secret place, I have eaten my heart'.*
> (I have not been deceitful).

and

> *'Hail, strider backwards, coming forth from Bast. I have not spoken against any man'.*

also

> *'I am the great cat, dwelling in the seat of right and truth.'*

With the establishment of Christianity as the state religion, echoes of the cult of Osiris were absorbed into the Coptic creed. Their gospel, the *Pistis Sophia* describes how the dead are judged within the body of the cosmic serpent. Several of the judges or their officers have cat faces.

The Christian afterlife is either Heaven, above the sky or Hell, below the earth. Hell (the name is taken from the Teutonic goddess of the dead, Hel whose animal is a cat. The concept of Hell is based on the Judaic Sheol). Hell is presided over by Satan, the Devil. He is alleged to have appeared in the form of a black cat at least a thousand times during the time of the witchcraft persecutions.

The Irish Celts envisaged the afterlife as a land of joy and youth, Tir-Nan-Og, which is situated at the western horizon in the Atlantic Ocean. The Welsh version is Annwn; located beneath the earth. In these lands dwell the faery folk, the dead and elemental beings. The mythology of Annwn bears a strong resemblance to the legend of Osiris.

Central to the Celtic religion was re-incarnation of the soul. The Celts therefore had no fear of death, which greatly upset Roman sensibilities on the battlefield. They could not understand the willingness of the Celts to put themselves in situations which demanded extreme bravery and which resulted in almost certain death. The Celtic Underworld could be seen through the eyes of a cat and those dwelling therein were able similarly to see out. The inhabitants of Tir-nan-Og/Annwn were able at will to pass between the worlds, mortals were sometimes abducted or inadvertently stumbled through an entrance to the Underworld. Return was difficult, a few hours in the Underworld was equivalent to several years in ours. To eat or drink in the Underworld was never to return at all.

Mummification of Cats

It says much for the Egyptian attitude to cats that hundreds of little cat mummies have been found at Sais and Bubastis. It appears, however, that some of them have been deliberately sacrificed to become votive offerings for worshippers at the temples. X-ray analysis confirms this. Such a practice conflicts with the overall attitude to cats, the killing of which incurred the death penalty.

Prince Tuthmosis who lived during the eighteenth dynasty had his cat mummified. She is shown as sitting at a table laden with gifts. Behind her stands her feline mummy. She is described as, 'Osiris, the Lady Cat'.

At Abydos, a small pyramidal tomb contains the bodies of seventeen cats. Small bowls were provided, thought to contain milk or food for their journey to the Underworld.

The Soul's Journey to the Underworld

The cat as an animal of boundaries has knowledge of the realms of the dead, or the Underworld. However dark, the cat always finds it's way. It's glowing eyes are able to illumine the darkness first encountered when passing through the boundaries between states of being.

The soul or 'ba' on it's way to the Underworld was offered refreshment by Hathor or Net from a sycamore-fig tree. The sycamore-fig was the Tree of Life and to partake of the fruit was to become one with the goddess and never return to earth. Persephone was unable to return to earth as she had eaten pomegranate seeds. This bound her to the Underworld for four months of the year. Both pomegranates and figs are symbols of fertility, due to their many seeds.

Tutankhamun is shown standing on the back of a black cat on his way to the Underworld. All dead heroes/gods are sought by their wives/mothers: Diana retrieved Lucifer, Freya, Frey and Isis, Osiris. All are connected with the cat.

Cats have been associated with death by most cultures: some say that the soul will go into the form of a cat, others that a cat will convey them to the other side.

In Malaya, the Jakur people believe that on death, their souls will be escorted to Paradise by a cat who will spray water on the fiery infernal regions to protect the soul from injury. The souls of Burmese monks were thought to enter cats where they remained until the cat itself died.

A Japanese cat with a black patch on it's back was thought to contain a dead soul. Such cats were sent to the temples for safe keeping.

East and west Africa have a taboo on killing cats - it is believed that souls of the dead are carried by them.

Far up in the north, Finnish people also believe that a cat would fetch their souls. An account is found in the epic poem, 'The Kalevala'.

A shaman entered a hut where men were resting. He sat down and began to intone spells. Almost immediately, the men found themselves in a sledge, pulled by a cat which took them swiftly to the limits of Pohjola (a land of darkness and spirits). They travelled as far as the deserts of Lapland, 'where the horse's footstep no longer resounds and the mare's foal finds no pasture'. The Norse goddess of love and war drove a sledge drawn by cats. She sought the souls of dead heroes on the battlefield.

The Celtic people believed that by looking into the cat's eyes, you could see into the land of faerie (which is a pleasanter version of the Underworld than the Classical or Greek version). In the story of Dermot and the Cat, the cat was symbolic of death and the power which would destroy the world.

Japanese burial rituals were complex and had to be performed to perfection. If this was not done, the soul of the deceased would return to wreak havoc on the relatives. Japanese fishermen would take a tortoiseshell cat with them on their boats at night to protect against the anger of 'honourable ancestors'.

In Europe, the soul's destination was determined by whether a cat climbed up or down a tree at the moment of death. If a white cat left the house the soul was bound for heaven. If a black cat left, then hope for salvation was lost. A rector was requested by a bereaved brother to pray for his sibling's soul which he believed was in hell. The rector, surprised, asked the man how he knew this to be so. The reply was that a white cat was seen coming down a tree at the moment of the brother's death.

There is a world-wide belief that cats should be kept away from a corpse. If the cat was allowed to pass across the body, it would become 'undead', a vampire. This belief is found in countries as far apart as Japan and Great Britain. The Japanese vampire cat had two tails and was therefore obvious.

Phantom cats are thought to herald a disaster, if not a death in the family. In 1902, Crown Princess Louisa of Saxony saw a ghostly black cat in the royal chapel in Zinzendorf Strasse, Dresden. Did this presage the destruction of that lovely city forty years later?

CHAPTER 7

THE ORIENTAL CAT

ll cats have an indefinable air of mystery about them and the Oriental cat has more than most. As we travel eastwards from Egypt, cats are still part of myth and legend with the exception of one or two areas. They are also still venerated (or cursed), according to the country in which they find themselves.

Israel is a close neighbour of Egypt and relations between the two have not always been cordial. The cat has no mention in the *Old Testament* of the *Bible* and records of cats as household animals are almost unknown.

The differences between the monotheistic religion of the Hebrew people and the polytheistic Egyptians could not have fostered understanding between the two cultures. The situation would not have improved when King Sheshonq invaded Israel during the era of Cat-worship in Egypt. As the greatest insult in Egypt was to obliterate all record of someone's existence (as the solar priesthood attempted to do after the fall of the Aten), perhaps the Hebrews were unwittingly delivering a subtle snub to their neighbours.

In Sinai, the cheetah and the serval were sacred to Hathor.

The Talmud mentions the cat. There are two versions of the Talmud: the Palestinian Talmud (c400 C.E.) mentions a ritual for clairvoyance and the other, the Babylonian Talmud (c500 C.E.), praises the cat, telling of it's usefulness in 'keeping the houses clean'. Ancient Persian legend maintained that the cat was born from the lion's sneeze. Neither the ancient Sumerian nor Babylonian religions had records of a cat-cult as such. Much later in time, with the establishment of Islam, the cat was greatly appreciated. There are many legends concerning the Prophet and the cat. A cat once saved the Prophet from almost certain death by snake bite. A cat always falls on its feet because Mohammed stroked it's back. The letter 'M' which appears between the ears of tabbies recalls the Prophet's fingers.

While living in Damascus, the Prophet had a cat called Muezza. One day the cat had curled up in the sleeve of his robe. Mohammed, not wishing to disturb his friend, cut away his sleeve. The Prophet was known to preach from the towers of Mecca, cradling his cat in his arms. The cat was so beloved by the Prophet that it is allowed to freely enter mosques. Cats are therefore treated kindly by Islam and it is illegal to kill them.

Greek legend tells of goddesses who have association with the cat, Diana, Demeter, Hecate and Venus. These associations have been dealt with elsewhere. Apart from these, the cat does not seem to have enjoyed a great popularity with the Greek culture, although the animal has appeared on coins. Aristotle mentions the cat in his 'History of Animals'. The Greeks preferred the mongoose to deal with their snakes and rodents. They also regarded the Egyptian religion with a smile and raised eyebrows. The situation does seem to have improved somewhat by

600B.C.E. when cats begin to figure in art and bones have been discovered. A Sicilian poet, C3rd century B.C.E. claims that the cat was established as a household pet on the island. A funerary stele on Salamis remembers a youth who died during the 5th century B.C.E. Engraved on the stele are a slave, a bird in a cage and a cat.

Further to the east, India seems to have taken the cat to it's heart. A cat skeleton has been found in the Indus valley and dated to about 2000B.C.E. but there is no way of determining whether it was a domestic animal or not. Cats often played an important part in the ritual of some religions. The Parsees respected the cat greatly and to kill one was considered a serious crime. It did not, however, attract the death penalty as in Egypt.

The Hindu word for cat is translated as 'the cleanser'. (Although the Sanskrit word for 'cat' and 'thief' are one and the same). One Hindu sect from southern India, has a doctrine which is based upon the way in which a cat behaves towards her young. It is believed that God saves a soul in the same manner in which a mother cat takes up her kittens. It disregards the free-will and represents salvation through grace. In contrast, a sect in the north of India uses the analogy of a monkey-mother to her young: that the soul is saved by holding to God's word as a baby monkey clings to it's mother.

Authorities differ as to the origins of the oriental cat as found in Burma, Malaya, Thailand, China and Japan. They are certainly revered and in some instances have been deified. In common with their western cousins, oriental cats show both extremes of personality and so we find both angelic and demonic cats in the myths and legends of these countries.

The Sacred Cat of Burma has been kept in temples of northern Burma for hundreds of years. This is the Birman, a long-haired animal which is not to be confused with the Burmese cat which is short-haired.

In the days before the coming of Gautama Buddha, cats were kept in the underground temple of Lao-Tsun, 'the Abode of the Gods'. Cats were sacred as they carried the souls of the dead. The high priest was a devotee of the goddess Tsun-Kyan-Kse, who presided over the journey of the soul after death. He had a cat called Sinh who was oracular and no decision was made without first consulting him.

Sinh's master daily sat in adoration at the feet of the golden goddess who had eyes of sapphire.

One day, invaders approached the temple. The priests gathered around the master at the foot of the goddess' statue to ask her protection. The high-priest died and at the moment his soul left his body, Sinh jumped onto his head.

The priests watched as the cat's fur turned to gold and it's eyes became a dazzling blue. It's paws and ears turned the brown of earth except where it's feet touched the silver hair of it's deceased master. The cat turned to face the entrance of the temple.

The invaders were repulsed. For seven days, the cat stood gazing at the statue of the goddess who had bestowed her colours upon him. He neither ate nor moved.

When the time came for a new high-priest to be chosen, the priests and their cats assembled and waited until the cats, bearing the souls of their dead masters, chose a successor.

All the temple cats turned white in her honour.

Thailand, formerly Siam has always been associated with exotic cats. There seem to be two types: the blue-eyed cat which we think of as 'Siamese' with a buff body and points in different shades of brown and the Korat with golden eyes.

Cats were accepted members of households hundreds of years ago in Thailand and there is a tradition that cats would stand on the shoulders of soldiers and yell if they saw a stranger (or enemy) approaching. As in Burma, the Siamese people believed that a soul entered the body of a cat and passed on to Paradise on the death of the cat host.

Some Siamese cats have a 'temple mark' at the nape of the neck. It is a reminder that a god once picked up a sacred temple cat and the imprint of his fingers have been seen on the cat's descendants since that time. The kink in the tail of many Siamese cats is to remind them of something they have forgotten.

On the death of the king of Siam, one of his cats would be put in the tomb with his body. The tomb had small holes left in the structure and when the cat escaped, it was believed that the king's soul had a new host. The cat was taken to the temple with much ceremony.

The Korat has been known in Thailand for centuries. The Korat's short coat is a silvery grey-blue and it's eyes, which are large, change in colour from blue at birth, to amber then a dazzling green-gold. They are known as Si-Sawat in Thailand and considered as bringers of good luck. They were also considered to be sacred. There is an account of black-coated, golden-eyed cats to be seen reclining on cushions in golden cages. Beside the cages incense burned and offerings of food left for them. A similarity to the Celtic cats.

Malaya, at the tip of the Thailand peninsula also venerated the cat. The Malayan Jakur people believe that the cat leads the soul of the deceased on a journey which takes them first through the infernal regions before reaching paradise. While passing through the former, the cat sprays the atmosphere with water to lower the temperature.

The archipelago of the south seas, Sumatra, Celebes, Java and Kota Gadang all have rituals which involve the cat in the production of rain. Details will be given in the section on weather.

Far to the north in China, the cat has once again become a deified animal. The god of the gathered harvest, Li-Shou, took the form of a cat to protect the grain from rodents. Li-Shou was a practical deity, not to be thought of as the spirit of the corn.

The cat-cult was unknown in southern China, where they are considered as being too lazy to catch mice, and they were therefore liable to find themselves made into the evening meal. In Gansu, in the north of the country, there was a cat-cult and a taboo that they should not be eaten. They are especially revered here for their mousing abilities.

The cat was a protector of the silk-worm industry. During the season for feeding the silk-worms, farmers would collect all the cats they could find. Failing a plentiful supply of the real thing, pictures of cats with staring eyes were placed all round the walls of sheds and barns. The image was deemed to be as effective as the cat itself - an idea which was also found in Egypt. These pictures were also used to keep evil spirits and ghosts away from the home.

In Chinese astrology, the cat is represented by the rabbit or hare. The word for octogenarian and cat are phonetically close, so the cat is used as a symbol for long life.

In common with other cultures, the Chinese believed that cats were supernatural animals which could detect ghosts or evil spirits. In some areas there is evidence of a cat-spirit which was worshipped. Not only could cats see these demons, but they could also be the demons themselves. For this reason, dead cats are never buried, their bodies are hung up in trees and in Taiwan, one can still see trees festooned with the bodies of cats. White cats are thought to be able to steal moonbeams.

Cat vampires are known. An example is found in the story of the Cat of Nabeshima, wherein a cat kills the favourite concubine of the prince and takes her form. When the prince visits her at night, he becomes weaker and weaker. The impostor is eventually spotted by a soldier who keeps watch by night, rendering the cat-woman powerless. She escaped into the countryside where she was eventually hunted down and killed.

Another belief is that of a cat-spectre. When the spectre killed anyone, the dead person's belongings gravitated to the spectre's home.

Japan has much in common with not only China, but also Europe when it comes to cat mythology.

Towards the end of the tenth century C.E., the Emperor Ichijo found five newly-born kittens in a corner of his palace. The day was auspicious, the tenth day of the fifth moon. From that time, cats enjoyed a period of reverence and kindness unrivalled anywhere except possibly in the days of the goddess Bastet in Egypt.

Maneko-Neko, the 'Beckoning Cat'

Their rodent-hunting skills endeared them to the silk-worm farmers, who, like their Chinese counterparts also believed that a mere image of a cat would be as effective in deterring rodents. A Japanese proverb says:

When rats infest the palace, the slowest cat is superior to the fastest horse'.

Cats have been kept in temples as sacred animals and a cat with a black patch on the back of it's head is considered especially so. The mark is thought to represent a woman in a kimono. A sixth century C.E. manuscript records sacrifices being made to the 'Guardian of the Manuscripts', a sacred cat who guarded papyrus rolls stored in temples against the ravages of mice and images of cats were placed in tombs to deter rats. One of the best known of these cats is the Nemuro-Neko, or Sleeping Cat, at the entrance of Ieyasu Tokugawa's tomb in Nikko. The cat is shown sleeping among peonies over the door to the shrine.

There is a shrine to a famous cat who once lived at the temple of Gotokuji, Tokyo.

Many years ago, the temple was no more than a poor hut, housing poverty-stricken monks. The monks had a cat with whom they shared what little food they had. One day, a company of Samurai horsemen approached. The cat watched them and raised a paw as if beckoning them. The horsemen stopped and entered the temple to shelter from the torrential rain which had just begun. They took tea and talked. The rain ceased and the Samurai left. One of them, Lord Li was moved by the monks and their simple faith. He returned and the temple eventually became the property of his family. The temple is now a shrine where people may seek help for their sick cats or continuing health and happiness. Ashes of dead cats are taken there.

Japanese Vampire-Cat

The Beckoning Cat, Maneki-neko, is to be found everywhere in Japan, especially outside shops and geisha houses. It is a popular talisman and is considered especially lucky for children.

There is a delightful study of cats by the artist Utagawa Kuniyoshi (1797-1861 C.E.). The work depicts cats representing staging posts on the Tokaido road. Legend records that at one of these posts, a witch would turn herself into a black cat and frighten women visiting the temple nearby. One day her wickedness worked against her, and she was turned into stone. The 'cat-stone' is still to be seen there. One of the illustrations shows a black cat confronting a short-tailed cat.

Supernatural cats, as in China, are the cause of much fear. In the Victoria and Albert Museum in London, there are some excellent examples of prints showing these cats which have enormous eyes. Mice are thought to be the souls of the dead, and Japanese fishermen will often protect themselves with a tortoiseshell cat aboard ship to deter rats and also their ancestors.

Cat vampires are specially feared in Japan. They can, however, be easily detected by having two tails. For this reason, the Bobtail cat is popular in Japan. It is similar to our native Manx cat, but is no relation. The Japanese version has been known for centuries.

'Thou Victim of my Paw'

CHAPTER 8

CAT AND MOUSE

'Thou victim of my paw,
By well-established law...'
Aesop.

The relationship between the cat and the mouse has been with us from the beginning of time. Legends abound with tales of the eternal struggle between victim and predator and the cat does not always come out the victor.

Cats and mice are also associated with the beginning of the world.

In Greek mythology, the mouse is sacred to Apollo, the god who had rulership over herds and flocks, prophecy, music, light and healing. As Apollo Smintheus, a mouse was kept near his statue in the temple at Hamaxitus, but there is no evidence for a mouse-cult.

Apollo wished to play a trick on his sister, Artemis. He gave much thought to his plan and conceived the idea of creating an animal very fierce and large which would challenge his sister as huntress and patroness of wild animals. He created the lion. The animal terrified man but Apollo did not reckon with his sister's bravery. Not only did she like the animal, but created a small replica, the cat. The other gods laughed and Apollo, perceiving a slight to his dignity, made a mouse. Artemis set her cat upon the little mouse and the rivalry has existed ever since.

In this myth, cats and mice represent the constant need to balance points of view. In order to learn and progress, new ideas must be challenged. Nothing must stagnate.

Legends of the flood also illustrate the beginning of the enmity between the two, the tale is similar from both Biblical and Islamic tradition.

At the flood, Noah took in pairs of mice and rats. Very soon he was over-run and the grain stores threatened. Noah asked the lion for his help. The lion sneezed and produced a pair of cats, thus solving Noah's problem.

Another version runs: God created the cat and the Devil, in an attempt to sink the ark, created the mouse. Very soon the mouse had nibbled a hole in the ark but was caught by the cat. A frog very obligingly crept into the hole and sealed it up.

There is another flood legend, this time from the Chippaway people from North America. In this version, a mouse stole a bag which contained the sun's heat and chewed it up to repair his shoes. The heat escaped through the hole in the bag and caused the snow to melt, flooding the earth.

Eclipses of sun or moon were thought to be the result of mice nibbling away at them. (Remember the moon being likened to cheese?). The Dakotan people believed that the waning moon was due to mice chewing it. The grey clouds of the evening sky were likened to mice which dispersed in the light of the (feline) moon.

In Egypt, the remedy for eclipses was to make as much noise as possible with sistra (the instruments of Hathor and Bastet) to awaken the solar cat.

The Zoroastrian religion regards mice as evil and to kill a mouse is equal in merit to the killing of four lions. Teutonic myth also usually sees the mouse as demonic.

Jewish tradition holds that eating anything gnawed by a mouse causes loss of memory. This, they believe, explains why cats cannot remember their masters. In Russia, Jewish children are forbidden to touch cats for this reason.

The ancient Egyptians believed that mice arose as if by magic from the fertile mud of the Nile. They credited the vulture and the scarab beetle with the same ability and all three were symbolic of life and fertility. Embalmed bodies of mice and shrew-mice have been found. The little shrew, the object of horror in Europe was considered in Egypt to be an incarnation of Horus.

It was the connection with the life-giving aspect which rendered them useful as a medicine. The earliest written record of a mouse as child's medicine, dating back to 1500B.C.E. Remains of mice have been found in the bodies of children buried c4000B.C.E. As a remedy for whooping cough, mice were used in Britain well into this century. Near Flamborough whooping cough was treated by wearing a nest of mice in a bag around the neck: as the mice died, they took the disease with them. In fact, mice cooked in any manner were considered useful in treating coughs, colds, sore throats, fevers and fits. Mouse blood was a sovereign cure for warts while a thread dipped in it and swallowed cured quinsy (abscess on throat).

Both Apollo, and his son Asclepius were healer-gods and they may have adopted the idea of the curative power of the mouse from both the ancient Egyptian beliefs. Mouse teeth were worn as protective charms.

Calling all ailurophobes - according to a tradition in Fishtoft, Lincolnshire, you do not need a cat to control mice. A window in the parish church shows St. Guthlac (a seventh century hermit of the area) holding a whip which was given to him by St. Bartholomew. As long as Guthlac holds the whip, Fishtoft will be free of rats and mice.

The ancient Irish bards also had a method of ridding themselves of rats and mice (the Celtic cat because of it's fierce nature was known to get rid of the bard as well). Poetry is a magical tool. Poetical ridicule was dreaded by king and noble alike. Rats were exterminated by a verse of satire and Shakespeare mentions it:

'I never was so be-rhymed since Pythagoras' time,
That I was an Irish rat -which I can scarcely
remember'.

Rosalind: *'As You Like It'.*

Seanchan Torpest, the Chief Ollave of Ireland made the mistake of satirising Irusan, the king of cats. Irusan was large and bore Torpest away to its home in Knowth where he nearly met a sad end. Cats do not have a sense of humour when directed against themselves.

No mouse gets past a vigilant cat. A Russian legend tells that Satan in the form of a mouse tried to slip past the dog and the cat who were guarding the gates of Heaven. He crept past the dog and was pounced on by the watchful cat.

In some parts of Europe, to rid oneself of their presence, one or two mice are caught and worshipped while others are burnt. This must have sent an extremely confusing message to the mouse population.

If rats and mice were pests in Europe, the little shrew was considered a demon. Cats will catch and kill them, but rarely eat the body because of the foul-tasting glands in the shrew's skin.

The bite of this diminutive creature was considered venomous and any contact was dangerous in the extreme. Topsell says of it:

> 'It is a ravening beast, feigning itself gentle and tame, but being touched it biteth deep and poysoneth deadly. It beareth a cruel mind desiring to hunt anything, neither is there any creature that it loveth'.

There may be some truth in Topsell's description. Shrews do not tolerate another in their territory, except at breeding times. If they should meet, they shriek at each other with loud, threatening squeaks which can be heard for some distance. To 'beshrew' someone was to curse and wish them evil. A spiteful, nagging woman was called a shrew and Shakespeare wrote a play on that subject, 'The Taming of the Shrew', which was a great success.

The shrew's reputation was such that in some parts of Britain it was very unlucky to meet one when setting out on a journey. Most people doing so would return home.

The shrew was supposed to visit dreadful inflictions on farm animals. A paralysis or numbing of limbs or spine was brought about by shrews running across the back or limb. In Scotland this was called Faery Riding and it is possible that the shrew may have been considered a faery animal. In both countries, the remedy was the same. A hole would be bored in a tree, preferably an ash tree. A live shrew would be put inside and the hole sealed up. Twigs and branches of this tree, which was now called a shrew-ash, would be gently drawn across the affected part.

There was a shrew-ash known as the Sheen Ash in Richmond Park, Surrey until 1895. Cattle, horses and children were brought to be healed. Another Ash stood near the parsonage in Warton, Lancs. The vicar had it uprooted, hoping this would have a similar effect on local belief.

Another plant which was said to bring relief was the root of the black or white thistle. There are several varieties of thistle, none of which are termed either black or white. Most of them are medicinal. The ash tree is considered both magical and medicinal so it is not surprising that it has been used for this purpose.

Another cure could be made from the genital of lamb or kid, mixed with hartwort and myrrh. Hartwort may be Aristolochia, which is used in the treatment of venomous bites and also known as Snakeroot. Tincture of myrrh is excellent for treating infected wounds and it's numbing action relieves pain. The genitalia may be to enforce the symbolism of life.

Failing the availability of either thistle or ash, it was the shrew itself which provided the cure.

Pliny recommends catching a shrew, letting it die and hanging the body round the neck of cattle.

Hippocrates gives a recipe for treatment of sores resulting from the bite of a 'mad' dog (rabid). The tail cut from a live shrew, made into an ointment and applied. The idea here is to fight like with like.

A remedy for the relief of piles is offered by Marcellus: Take a dead shrew from cart track or path. Burn it and mix ashes with goose-grease.

A shrew was supposedly blind and it was thought that it would die if it attempted to cross a path or trackway. Perhaps the shrew's 'medicinal qualities' and it's supposed blindness gave rise to the following nursery-rhyme:

> Three blind mice, three blind mice,
> See how they run, see how they run,
> They all ran after the farmer's wife
> Who cut off their tails with a carving knife,
> Did you ever see such a thing in your life,
> As three blind mice?

Both cats and mice have been symbolic of, or were vehicles of, the human soul in various cultures. Artemis (feline moon) is the 'Madonna of the Silver Bow', huntress of men's souls (mice). According to Breton and German tradition, the soul in this form leaves the body through the mouth.

On the island of Celebes in the West Indies, mice as souls of the dead, and especially that of a suicide are dangerous as they will eat the rice and take away it's soul. It follows that mice are also thought to be harbingers of death and will leave a house at the death of the master; (similar to rats deserting a sinking ship). Mice running across anyone, sick or well warned of death as did a mouse squeaking behind a sick-bed. In Flensburg, northern Germany a white mouse is said to foretell death whereas in Bohemia, a white mouse must not be killed: it should be taken from the trap, fed and allowed to run free otherwise bad luck will come upon the house.

In Japan, fishermen will take a tortoiseshell cat with them on board their boats, not only to protect them from rats, but also to deter the 'honourable ghosts' of their ancestors.

There have been times when rats have proved to be friends to humanity.

Ptah, the husband of Bastet's sister Sekhmet, helped the Egyptians to defeat the Assyrians by instructing rats to creep into Assyrian tents at night and chew their bowstrings. The cat was barred from Buddha's funeral because it ate the rat who had been dispatched to fetch the Buddha's medicine.

The cat did not always have things his own way: an Egyptian papyrus from the nineteenth dynasty shows a battle between cats and rats. The rats seem to be winning. The Rat Pharaoh leads in a chariot drawn by dogs against a fort defended by the cats.

A tale from fourteenth century Persia tells of a battle between cats and rats wherein the rats seem to be on the point of surrendering when the cat leader falls from his horse, is captured and the cat army runs away in terror.

In English churches, there are misericords which depict rats hanging a cat: two examples are to seen in the Priory Church of Great Malvern and Worcester Cathedral.

A case of witchcraft during the early part of this century also turns the tables on puss.

One Jabez Few was thought to practice witchcraft. He kept several white mice as pets and the villagers assumed these to be his familiars. One day, for whatever reason, Few put one of his mice into a woman's bedroom. To get rid of it, the woman put a large tomcat inside the room. Sounds of furious fighting were heard. When the door was opened, the cat was seen to be clinging to the curtains and the mouse was unharmed. When Jabez Few died, his nephew could only dispose of the mice by holding them over running water - they scuttled away and were not seen again. Running water is sure defence against psychic attack: spitting may have it's origins here.

Another witch, one Thomasina Read of Haddenham, in Cambridgeshire, confessed that the Devil came to her in the form of a mouse. She asked that he would blast a nearby village, which he apparently did as the inhabitants later suffered from fits. Thomasina denied nothing at her trial, but was eventually acquitted.

The cat versus mouse dilemma is played out on our television screens in the guise of Tom and Jerry.

Look carefully at the way in which the two characters are portrayed: Tom is neither black nor white, his two extreme natures have been blurred into grey. He is 'toned down', never to be perfectly good nor yet to be extremely wicked (and kill Jerry). Jerry is not grey like the usual house-mouse. He is brown, in common with hamsters, gerbils and similar 'cuddly' little animals.

The story line examines the love/hate relationship between the two: Tom stalks upon Jerry who runs for his life. Being small he has to use his wits and this is when poor Tom generally comes off the worse. There is a meaning here that we must never underestimate the opposition, however impossible the odds may seem to be against them. Neither should we give up without trying: we all have secret reserves of strength and initiative.

Tom's teeth are only sharp and threatening when he believes himself to have got away with murder (which he never manages to do). When he is caught by the housekeeper, he grins sheepishly and his teeth are human teeth. Jerry is not always as good as he would have us believe him to be. He steals food if he can get it. When Tom (doing his job) tries to catch him, pandemonium breaks out, Jerry vanishes and Tom is punished for his trouble. Tom just cannot win, either indoors or out where the dog seizes the slightest opportunity to attack him. There is nothing subtle about the dog whose 'always-carnivorous' teeth leave us in no doubt as to what would happen to Tom if he were caught.

This is violence on a grand scale. If it were a wildlife documentary, there would be public outrage and rightly so. However much we love our cats, 'Tom and Jerry' is only a cartoon, we may laugh until our sides ache: it is life turned on it's head, a reversal of the norm. David and Goliath. A kind of fifteen minute Saturnalia in front of the television. It does, however, hint to us that we can win, no matter what the odds; if a problem appears insurmountable, turn it upside down to find the answer.

The cat and mouse archetypes are to be seen everywhere in our society: how often do we hear someone described as 'catty' or 'mousy?'

'Cattiness' is applied to people who manage to do with words what a spiteful cat manages with it's claws. It is the power of the tongue to wound another and because the comment is often 'witty', the memory and the hurt last far longer than the situation merits. (Hence the affront to Irusan due to Torpest's satirical verses). Shy, insecure folk are sometimes described as 'mousy'. These people may have low self-esteem and back down at the first sign of argument or threat.

Unfortunately, the cat archetype is drawn to them; there is something about timidity which invites aggression and bullying. The cat is stimulated by movement, a mouse once caught is left alone until it moves, then the paw falls on it. What if the mouse were to stand his ground and remain still? (Or, as happened to the cat of a friend, the mouse jump up and nip the cat's nose?). It is not easy to stand up to bullies, but they do back down surprisingly quickly.

CHAPTER 9

THE CELTIC CAT

The Celtic civilisation of Britain and north-west Europe was at it's height from about 500B.C.E. to the Roman conquest. As a cultural group, they were probably established several thousand years earlier.

Celtic tradition was handed down by word of mouth and no written records remain. Such tales as we do have were not put to paper (or parchment) until well into the Christian era, nevertheless, the tales are of great antiquity and reveal a highly sophisticated religious and moral culture.

The Celtic cat differs from other cats in this work in that it is descended from a different species of animal. The African Wild Cat (Felis lybica), which proved friendly to man did not arrive at our shores until comparatively recently, either with the Phoenician traders or the Romans.

The cat which permeates the Celtic legends, may be the European Wild cat (Felis sylvestris). I use the term, 'may' because the cats of Celtic myth are large and black. The indigenous wild cat, now found only in the Highlands of Scotland, has a similarity to the tabby, dark stripes with a thick, blunt-ended tail. They are larger than the domestic cat, males having a body length of three feet plus a twelve inch tail. These cats generally breed only once a year, during May; and this may have some bearing on the reputation of May cats. They are extremely aggressive, avoiding contact with man. If captured they remain hostile and even tiny kittens become savage as they mature.

The cat of legend is very similar to large black cats seen all over mainland Britain. Sightings of these animals have been recorded since the turn of the century and not only in remote areas. Some have been seen in the home counties. Some authorities believe that these cats are not, as was suggested, escapees from circus and zoo, but an indigenous species which are seen now because of man's intrusion into their world. There is much to commend this exciting theory.

Deities connected with the British cat-cult exhibit the same degree of ferocity as the cat itself.

One of the most fearsome was Black Annis, a goddess worshipped in the Dane Hills area of Leicestershire. She was described as 'a savage woman with long, tattered hair, great teeth and long nails' She was also known as 'Cat Annis'. Annis is thought to be the English name of the Danaan goddess, Ana. In which case, Annis would represent the maleficent aspect of Ana as a member of the triplicity of Ana, Badb and Macha known as the Morrigan. It has also been suggested that Annis is another form of the goddess Yngona, a well-known Danish goddess. Whatever the truth, Black Annis is a fearsome hag and was probably worshipped in the area long before the Danish invasions.

Black Annis haunted a grove of oak trees, similar to Diana of Ephesus. It is possible that Annis was originally connected with tree-worship, similar to the hag who is said to inhabit elder trees. Black Annis demanded human sacrifice, preferably children. Children who stayed outside after dark were warned by their parents that Black Annis would catch them, skin them alive and devour them. Scattering their bones and hanging their skins to dry in her oak tree. To this day, it is common to hang pieces of cloth on sacred trees to obtain favours.

Black Annis' Bower is a cave said to be scratched out of the hillside by her claws.

The Gaelic language has eight words for 'cat'. One of them, 'puss' we have taken into the English language.

The Druidic priesthood of Ireland performed a ritual known as 'Imbas Forosnai' to see into the future. The ritual consisted of chewing the raw flesh of a cat, (sometimes it was that of a dog or pig), which had been sacrificed to the appropriate deity. This act is well-documented in Celtic lore. The hero Finn burnt his thumb whilst cooking the Salmon of Linn Feic. He put his thumb into his mouth to cool the pain and chewed it down to the bone. Insight came to him. The Welsh Taliesin also put his thumb into his mouth when scalded with three drops of Cerridwen's brew. He also received the gift of knowledge.

The chief Ollave of Ireland, Seanchan Torpest incurred the wrath of the Cat King, Irusan. Torpest wrote a slanderous verse about Irusan who snatched the Ollave up and bore him away. Irusan was reputed to be 'as large as an ox' and lived at Knowth.

Cats contended with heroes in many forms Cuchulainn and two companions were attacked in a cave one night by three magical cats which disappeared when the sun rose. One cat

110

stretched it's neck out and Cuchulainn struck at it with his sword. The weapon bounced off as if it had hit stone. Other cats in Celtic myth had two or ten tails and others could sting badly. It was believed that if you trod on a cat's tail, a serpent would appear and sting you.

In the ancient kingdom of Connaught in north-west Ireland was a Cat shrine at Clogh-magh-righ-cat. This cat was black, lithe and slender. It gave prophecy while reclining on a throne of old silver. Should the cat suspect that the questioner was being facetious in some way, the answer would be scathing.

The Aitheach-Tuatha, a pre-Gaelic race who overthrew the Milesians, set a cat-eared king over the vanquished people. This was Cairbre Cinn-cait (Cairbre of the Cat Head) of whom the poet Eochaid ua Floinn says,

> *Thus was Cairbre the Cruel,*
> *who seizes Ireland south and north,*
> *two cat's ears on his fair head*
> *and cat's fur through his ears'.*

Epithets attached to heroes and mythological beings generally refer to an outstanding attribute, a physical curiosity or reference to a totem or god figure. Cairbre may therefore have worn a catskin over his head in allegiance to his deity or totem animal. He may indeed have had the ears of a cat. Many kings in ancient legend were reputed to have had animal ears: King Mark of Cornwall had horses' ears and King Midas had the ears of an ass. The story of Morann Mac Main's Collar seems to refer to the latter, as each son which was born to Cairbre was so-marked, so he killed them.

From the *Book of the Dun Cow* (circa 1100 C.E.), comes the story of an incident during the Voyage of Maeldun.

Maeldun was the son of an Irish chief who had been murdered by raiders. Accompanied by several companions and his foster-brothers, Maeldun sailed in pursuit and came to the Island of the Little Cat.

By this time, the men were starving, as the apples they had brought with them had long since been eaten. Before them the island rose like a white tower. On the ramparts were white houses. Hoping to find refreshment, the company entered one of the dwellings. A little cat playfully leapt between four stone pillars. It looked at the men, but carried on with it's game. On the walls of the room were hung jewels, necklaces and brooches. On the floor, warm clothes and before the hearth a side of bacon, some roast beef and a skin of wine.

Maeldun turned to the cat and asked, 'Is this for us?'

The cat looked at him, said nothing and continued it's game.

The warriors sat down, partook of the feast, drank the wine and fell asleep. In the morning as they were leaving, one of the company, Maeldun's foster-brother, took a piece of jewellery from the wall. The cat suddenly changed into a fiery arrow and shot straight through the man who fell to the floor in a heap of ashes.

Maeldun, greatly shocked, apologised to the cat, replaced the necklace and left. The dead man's ashes were scattered on the shore and the heroes put to sea again.

This cat represented fire as retribution, as did Sekhmet/ Hathor when sent to punish humanity by Ra. Cats are notorious thieves, was this an example of the adage, 'Set a thief to catch a thief'?

Another Irish tale involving the cat is of Dermot and his companions, Goll, Conan and Oscar.

The companions had finished a day's hunting when night began to fall and they sought shelter.

They found a hut and on entering found an old man, a young girl, a cat and a wether. They were offered hospitality and as they sat at table, the wether jumped upon it. One by one, the heroes tried to lift the sheep from the table, failing, exhausted. Finally Goll managed to push it from the table, but ended up on the floor beneath it. The old man asked the cat to lead the wether back to it's stall.

The heroes were humiliated and decided to leave. The old man restrained them, 'There is no shame', he said, 'The wether is the world, the cat is death, which will destroy the world'. The old man represented the passing of time.

That night, the maiden was approached by the heroes and refused them all. To each, she said, 'I was yours once and can never be again. For I am youth'. To Dermot she said, 'The same is for you - but I will give you a mark by which every woman will love you.'

She touched his brow and the mark she left drew the love of women for as long as he lived.

Gaelic legend does not always give the cat a good name, but here is a story of an Irish Faery cat with a happy ending:

A poor old woman would sit late into the night spinning. One cold evening there came a knock at her door. Frightened, she asked who knocked,

Ach, Judy. Let us in for I'm cold and hungry'.

She opened the door slowly and through the gap came a black cat with two white kittens. The old woman sat down again, saying not a word. The cats sat at her fire warming themselves and washing.

Finally, the black cat spoke to Judy, telling her to go to her bed as she had already hindered the faeries' business enough for one night.

'If it hadn't been for me and mine,' said the cat, 'you would be dead by now. But fetch us a bowl of milk and be gone to your bed'.

Judy fetched the milk and set it before them. The cats drank it up and suddenly shot up the chimney. As she looked, Judy saw something shining in the ashes. A silver coin, left for her kindness; it was sufficient to enable her to give up working late at night. She never did so again.

Scotland has mythology which is similar to that of it's southern neighbour, England. North of the border it is the Cailleach Bheur, the Blue Hag of Winter that takes cat-form. She was a shape-shifter, like the Welsh Cerridwen. The Isle of Mull, scene of the dreadful Taigheirm, has cat-like demons and witches in the Scottish Highlands turn themselves into black, savage cats.

Tales are told of elfin cats, 'Cait Sith', described as large and black with arched backs, erect bristles and a white spot over the chest. There are also faery cats which were dark green in colour with very long ears.

There are single standing-stones in Scotland which are known as 'cat stanes'.

The Silurian people of south-east Wales worshipped a cat. They believed that, by looking into a cat's eyes, the Otherworld could be seen. The cat's eyes were, indeed the windows of the Faery King's domain. By looking through them, the faeries could look out and the mortals in.

The Welsh Hag-Goddess, Cerridwen has a link with the cat-cult through her son, Taliesin and as being the mother of the fiercesome Cath Palug. Cerridwen was worshipped as long ago as 800B.C.E. but in the story of Cath Palug, King Arthur is involved. King Arthur is now thought to be placed around 600C.E., when Christianity was an established religion in Britain. The time lapse must be due to the oral tradition of Wales being maintained without regard to the time or a legend revived in which a pagan goddess is discredited.

As a child, Gwion was set to watch Cerridwen's cauldron. The brew inside was intended for her son, Agddu (the ugly). As the brew bubbled, a drop of the liquid fell onto Taliesin's hand, scalding him. He naturally put his thumb into his mouth to cool the burn and instantly received knowledge of the world, past and future.

115

Cerridwen was furious and pursued the lad mercilessly. They both changed their forms: she into the predator, he into the pursued. Finally he changed himself into a grain of wheat and she swallowed him. Nine months later, Gwion was reborn as Taliesin.

Taliesin, in describing his previous incarnations says,

'I have been a cat with spotted head upon a tripod'.

He also says:

'The spotted cat shall be disturbed, together with her men of a foreign language'.

The 'spotted cat' sounds very similar to the Scottish spotted cat referred to earlier. Perhaps this refers to an invasion from the north. To take speculation further, the animal may have been brought to our shores by Phoenician traders which then allows for the animal to be leopard or cheetah. Even the Egyptian wild cat which was spotted.

Note that the cat is referred to as 'she'. This may be the choice of gender used arbitrarily by the writer, or 'she' could be a queen or woman of authority who wears a catskin as part of her regalia.

Cerridwen was the mother of both Taliesin and a savage cat. Perhaps the cat was the alter-ego of Taliesin. (As Sekhmet was of Bastet). In speaking of previous incarnations, Taliesin equates himself with the sun. Should one of his incarnations have been in Egypt, he could be equating himself with the cat of Ra. The 'spotted cat upon a tripod' could be an idol: the Egyptian cat was spotted.

This is pure conjecture on the part of the writer. Unfortunately, the poem is incomplete and we can only guess at what is meant.

Cerridwen, Goddess of Life, Death and Shape-Shifting also appears in ancient legend as Henwen, the 'Old White One': the mystical sow. The account of Cath Palug begins in Kernyw (Cornwall), where Henwen was guarded by Coll, son of Collfrewr. Coll was one of the three chief enchanters of the Isle of Prydain.

It was prophesied that her offspring would bring trouble to Britain. She, sensing a threat to her purpose bolted to the coast at Awstin, swam across the sea to south Wales with Coll still clinging to her. She came ashore at Caldicot in Gwent, where the river Troggy pours into the Severn.

At Maes Gwenith (Field of Wheat), Henwen deposited a grain of wheat and a bee. At Llonwen in Pembrokeshire, she left a grain of barley and a bee. She then ran to Rhiw Gyferthwch in Snowdonia she brought forth a wolf-cub and an eagle chick. Coll gave the wolf-cub to Menwaed of Arllechwed and the eagle to the Goidel Brynach from the North.

Henwen then went to Maen Du (Black Stone) in Arfon and gave birth to a kitten. Coll threw the kitten into the Menai Straits whence it was fished out again by the sons of Paluc. It was this last gift by Henwen which was one of the Three Plagues of Anglesea.

During her journey, Henwen gives grain for man's use, showing her benevolent side. The grain and birth of a kitten link her with fertility Goddesses, such as Cat-Demeter.

Cath Palug was ferocious -

'Nine score fierce (men) fell for it's food.
Nine score warriors'.

The monstrous cat was killed by the warrior, Cei Wynn, who was later to become Sir Kay, a knight of the Round Table.

Cath Palug is recounted in the exploits of King Arthur and parallel legends from Europe. From a fourteenth century manuscript, 'Le Roman de Merlin', comes the following. It bears striking similarities to the Welsh version.

Whilst fishing in Lake Geneva, a man brought up a black kitten. He took it home, fed it and very soon it had outgrown all the other cats. It then killed the fisherman and his family.

The cat sought the mountains,

> *'a catte, full of the devell that is so grete and oughy, that it is a horrible sight on to loke'.*

King Arthur and his companions, guided by Merlin set out to rid the land of this terror. Merlin, knowing where the animal lived, whistled and the cat appeared and attacked Arthur. The fight raged all day, the cat crushing weapons in it's jaws and the king hacking the animal's limbs. Finally Arthur triumphed and slew the cat. The mountain on which the cat lived was renamed from 'Mont du Lac' to 'Mont du Chat'.

This version of the cat legend is also known as the *Cat of Lausanne*. Sometimes the Lake is not Geneva, but Lake Bourger in the French Alps.

In the '*Romanaz de Franceis*', Arthur fought the cat Capalu in a swamp. It killed him then went to England where it became king. This was not a version of the legend to be told in British baronial halls, but was probably of immense popularity in Europe.

The legend of Ogier the Dane dates from the ninth century. Ogier was the son of Duke Godfrey. Ogier has mystical connections: at his birth, Morgan le Fay took him to Avalon where he stayed for two hundred years at the end of which time he returned to the world to attack Christendom. Whilst on a voyage, he was shipwrecked on a small island in the Mediterranean Sea. Here he fought with a ferocious cat, known as the Capalus. He also fought with both King Arthur and Sir Gawain (being representatives of Christendom). Ogier returned to Avalon, where he and Morgan had a son called Meurvin. As the name sounds suspiciously like our 'Merlin, could this be the Medieval-European origin of his birth. In the '*Bataille Loquifer*', there is a youth called Kapalu, who is a servant of Morgan. This is similar to the Greek legend of Galinthias, who was banished to the Underworld in the form of a cat where she served as a priestess to Hecate.

The legendary ferocity of the cat is found in heraldry, where under the name cat-a-mountain or cat-a-mount, it appears on the arms of a few of the Scottish and Irish families. It is less frequently found in English heraldry.

The 'King of Cats' is frequently referred to in Celtic legend. (Mention has already been made of Irusan). On the Isle of Man he is an ordinary cat by day. At night he becomes his royal self and travels rapidly across country. Those who treated him unkindly during the day could expect to regret their treatment of him at night.

There is the story of two Englishmen who had rented a hunting lodge in the Highlands of Scotland. One day, one of the hunters felt unwell and remained behind while his friend went hunting. The friend returned late and over supper spoke of the day's events. He was lost in a wood and saw a light ahead. Thinking to ask directions, he followed it only to find it came from a hollow oak tree. At this point he broke off his account and pointed to the old cat sitting between them on the hearth.

'Look at that cat', he said, *'I swear it's listening to every word'*.

He continued: On looking into the tree, he saw a funeral taking place. All the mourners were cats. At these words, the hearth cat leapt up and exclaimed, 'At last! Old John's dead. Now I'm King of Cats'. He shot up the chimney and was never seen again. Dildrum is the name of another King of Cats who also vanishes up the chimney. The chimney is the usual exit for beings with Otherworld connections: witches and Father Christmas also use it.

If the Celtic 'cat cult' did venerate these animals as deities or sacred to deities, then the 'God of the Old Religion' did indeed become the 'Devil of the New Religion'. Later centuries were to personify the Devil as a black cat and his congregation were believed to turn themselves into cats and to keep cats for magical purposes.

Earlier this year, a television programme, 'Encounters' (Channel 4) gave an interesting documentary about sightings of the 'Beast of Exmoor'. The Ministry of Agriculture, Fisheries and Food agreed to launch an official investigation into the matter. The result of their investigations was published on July 20th. They concluded that the panther-like cat does not exist and the animals

120

sighted were only domestic cats. Disappointing, and I for one am not convinced. There is too much evidence. At the time of going to press, a large feline skull has been discovered in a river bed which constantly floods............For anyone interested in following up this line of enquiry, the following books are relevant as well as being a good read:

Bord, Janet & Colin: *'Alien Animals'* Panther Books. 1985

Francis, Di. *'Cat Country'* David & Charles. 1983

CHAPTER 10

THE TIDE TURNS

W hen the collapse of the Roman Empire occurred in the 5th century C.E. the legions withdrew, leaving just three things behind them: Five thousand miles of roads, the importance of the city and - Celtic Christianity. Unlike Gaul to the south, the Roman civilisation crumbled away in Britain. But the status of the cat remained.

With the establishment of Christianity, relations between the cat and the new faith were quite amicable. The early Celtic Church smoothed the path of conversion by accepting and adapting many pagan traditions where these did not conflict with the new teachings. Ancient deities too, were 'sanctified' and brought within the domain of the Church. St. Brigid of Ireland is as popular a saint now as she was beloved as a Mother Goddess several thousand years ago.

Reverence for the natural world was an integral part of the daily life of the Celtic Church and there are some beautiful passages and prayers which reflect this. There are several saints of this period who are associated with cats.

One is Saint Gertrude of Nivelles (626-59C.E). St. Gertrude's cult was particularly popular in the Low Countries. She is usually associated with mice, which has never been explained. It is possible that she took over attributes of a local pagan deity. She was invoked against the pestilence of rats and mice and offerings of gold and silver mice were left at her shrine in Cologne. Gertrude is depicted in art either holding a mouse or with a cat near her. She is the patroness of cats, gardeners, widows and travellers. She is particularly popular with those who are afraid of mice. (Too late, alas, for Julius Caesar, but his fear did not prevent him from building an Empire).

The Sicilian saint, Martha, is another lady associated with cats. She is the patron saint of household order and cleanliness and her animal is the cat. Both Martha and Gertrude stress the need for cleanliness. (The Hindu word for cat means 'cleanser').

St. Agatha (d 250C.E.) is of particular interest. She was invoked against storms and hail. On her feast day, 5th. February, church bells were rung to prevent bad weather. Women were supposed to refrain from work on St. Agatha's day. To those who were caught doing so, the saint appeared as an angry cat. In the south of France, St. Agatha is Santo Gato (St. Cat).

St. Jerome (341-420C.E.) was a monk and Doctor of the Church. St. Jerome was a learned and clever man, unfortunately of very difficult disposition and who managed to anger those with whom he came into contact. He lived a solitary life of study and is often depicted in art in the company of a cat or a lion. One painting of 'St. Jerome in his Study' in Venice shows a dog. The animal was originally a cat which has been overpainted. It is said that St. Jerome detested women as much as he liked animals.

My Friend, Pangur Ban

From south Wales comes St. Cadoc. He is associated with handing a cat to the Devil in repayment for the Devil's help in building a bridge. The motif of the Devil building a bridge and claiming for himself the first living thing to cross over is widespread in European myth.

The Devil was originally sent by God (we are told) to test and try mankind's integrity. By building bridges, mankind was offered an 'easy option' by crossing it, the alternative was to take the arduous journey the long way round. By offering the Devil a substitute, man was evading the Devil's trick: only the first to cross became his. Man, however, incurred a karmic debt by playing 'catspaw' with the cat: making the animal do the 'dirty work' and reaping the benefits for himself. The bridge also offers the choice of return to the Old Religion (The pagan deities having now been equated with Satan by the Church). The first to cross has therefore 'rejected' God and belongs to the Devil. The cat is handed over as 'belonging' to the Old Ways. This trick did not always work out as expected:

There is a town in France, just to the south-west of Orleans, called Beaugency. The Devil built the townspeople a bridge across the Loire, exacting the usual tribute. The Devil was handed a cat. Angrily, he tried to demolish the bridge, but the cat scratched his face and hands. The Devil dropped the cat who high-tailed it to Sologne, where it hid. This locality has since been called Chaffin, (Chatfin) or 'cat-end' and the good folk of Beaugency were called 'cats'.

By the ninth century, cats were highly valued in Britain and almost every household kept one and to harm or kill a cat was punishable by a fine of two pence.

An Irish monk of the same period wrote a poem about his little white cat called Pangur Ban. The poem is inserted in

Cats from a Medieval Bestiary

the pages of a manuscript which he was copying at the time. It gives a lovely picture of a man who loved his cat so much that he took time to leave a memento of him for later generations to read.

Cats were the only animals permitted to be kept in monasteries and convents: An 'Ancren Riwle of 1205 states:

'Ye, my dear sisters, shall have no beast but a cat'.

There is a Celtic Cross in a churchyard in Monasterboice in County Louth. On it's base are two cats: one licking a newly-born kitten and the other holding a bird in her paws. The symbology here may remind us that life and death are inextricably entwined. There is also a possibility that the cats refer to a far more ancient concept of the Mother Goddess who gives life and takes it. She is complete in herself

These were the good times for the cat in history.

With the passing of the Empire, the organising genius of the Romans was transferred to the Roman Church. The lack of cohesion in the Celtic peoples which rendered them vulnerable to conquest also weakened the Celtic Church. Although there was a measure of unity, the Celtic Churches tended to remain independent of each other and this resulted in limiting their influence both in Britain and Europe.

The Roman Missionaries were not pleased at what they found in the British Isles and set to with a will to reform matters. The Roman clergy left no doubt in the minds of the British, whether pagan or convert, that they were to be God's New Brooms and set about with the energy of the fanatic to obliterate all vestiges of paganism.

What was not obliterated was denounced as demonic. The ancient deities which were still 'outside' the new faith, had the dubious title of 'devil' thrust upon them.

The Church authorities adopted not only the words (if not always the spirit) of Jesus of Nazareth but also the teachings of the *Old Testament*. It is to this Book and the *New Testament* that we turn to seek references which may shed light on the later attitude of the Church towards the cat.

There are none.

There is no word meaning 'cat' in Biblical Hebrew. There are no references to the domestic cat in either the Old Testament or the New. This could mean that cats were not usually kept as domestic animals during the Biblical period; although the animal was depicted in domestic art by 1700B.C.E.

There is also the fact that the Jews, having been taken into slavery by the Egyptians had learned much of their captor's religious beliefs. The worship of Bast as a goddess of motherhood, erotic love and happiness contrasted sharply with their beliefs. There are references in the *Old Testament*, however, to Bubastis and the temple there.

The cat is mentioned in other Rabbinical literature however:

> 'Had the Torah not been given to us for our guidance, we would have learned modesty from the cat, honesty from the ant, chastity from the dove and good manners from the cock'.

From the *Apocrypha, (Letters of Jeremiah)*: (The *Apocrypha* is not considered a part of the Hebraic *Bible*)

'When their faces are blackened by the smoke of the temple, they are unaware of it. Bats and swallows and birds of all kinds perch on their heads and bodies and cats do the same. From this you may be sure that they are not gods, so have no fear of them'

There are instructions in the Jewish Talmud for obtaining clairvoyance:

'The eyes of a black cat, mixed with the gall of a man endowed with second sight'.

As the cat was not specifically mentioned in the Bible, European imagination soon filled the vacancy in Christian lore and legend.

Pictures depicting the Fall of Man in the Garden of Eden often include a cat. Eve was the second wife of Adam. His first wife was Lilith, but she repelled his advances and was expelled from Paradise. In medieval demonologies, she was depicted as being a beguiling woman with the clawed feet of a bird. However, a Sefardim legend believed that she became a black cat, known as El Broosha. Whatever her ultimate form, she was a vampire which preyed principally on children.

An engraving by Durer shows the cat sitting at Eve's feet while she samples the forbidden fruit. The cat symbolises that the choice has been made, for good or ill. Another picture painted by Frans Floris shows the cat in a central position between Adam and Eve. Here the cat has not favoured one or the other, but invites each to decide. Perhaps Durer was following the attitude of his time towards woman: that she and the cat were not to be trusted in contrast with the innocence of Adam.

An Italian legend tells that when Christ was born, a cat gave birth to a kitten at the same time, beneath the manger in which he was laid. Christ is linked with ancient solar cults of the dying (sacrificed)/resurrected God. One of his titles is 'Light of the World' which may thus be taken metaphorically. This also echoes the pagan tradition of a hero being born at the same time as a companion animal, (the Mabinogion tells of the birth of a foal at the same time as Pryderi). Boy and animal leading a mutually dependent life, the actions of one affecting the fortune of the companion.

Christ's Mother as a virgin is linked with Virgin Mother Goddesses such as Mut and therefore also has a link with the cat. The manger was a form of the cat's cradle, holding the Sun.

Cats appear in masterpieces depicting scenes with the Holy Family. Leonardo da Vinci included a kitten in many of his sketches and in Baroccio's painting of 'Madonna of the Cat', the infant John the Baptist is shown teasing a ginger-and-white kitten with a bird: birds represent the soul, so is John implying that though Jesus and the kitten (the Devil in disguise?) are yet young, later there will be a struggle for the souls of men? Cats and kittens in these pictures are reminiscent of the kitten born under the manger, innocent and playful.

In pictures of the Last Supper an adult cat is seen at the feet of Judas. A fresco by Ghirlandajo shows Judas with a cat, sitting alone. 'Last Supper' by Luini depicts Judas, with a striped cat at his feet, holding his silver reward.

Here the cat symbolises treachery: the kitten born with Jesus has turned traitor and brought about the downfall of his Companion. In so doing, he has brought about the downfall of himself as well, as we shall see. These works of art illustrate the prevailing attitude towards the cat. Do not forget, there is no Biblical precedent for or against the cat.

Throughout Europe, and continuing well into the seventeenth century, cats were thrown onto fires during the Lenten season: Shrove Tuesday, Good Friday and Easter Day. It would appear that the poor cat could not be made to suffer enough for it's 'complicity' with Judas.

In the Ardennes area, shepherds drove their flocks through the smoke and flame as a security against witchcraft. At Wambeck, 'evil' was expelled by throwing a cat out of the village. A Shrovetide custom was held in Shropshire where a cat was whipped to death to drive out the sins of the community:

> 'The finest pastime that is under the sun
> is whipping the cat at Albrighton'

This later became a way of teasing gullible strangers. Travellers were told that the local cats were strong enough to pull a man across the river. A rope was attached to a cat and the other end held by the visitor on the opposite bank. Villagers pretended to whip the cat and while the visitor's attention was distracted, he was pulled into the river.

The Conquest of England by William of Normandy brought with it increased control by the Church of secular as well as ecclesiastical matters. The age of Abbey and Church building began. Some churches dating from this period depict feline demons glaring from the tops of pillars. During the reign of Henry III (1216-1272 C.E.), cats had multiplied to the point where the king authorised cat hunting to control their numbers and provide the monks with furs. (I wonder what Pangur Ban's friend would think of that?)

It was the thirteenth century C.E. that Europe saw the rise of religious sects which disagreed with Rome's interpretation of the Bible, and sought a simpler, more fundamental approach to the Christian religion and thus earning for themselves the dreaded title of Heretic.

In pre-Christian times, heresy had no dark meaning, but St. Paul, in his letter to the Galatians (*Galatians 5:20*), condemns heresy together with idolatry and sorcery. From that time on it came to mean any religious belief or practice contrary to established orthodoxy. Many sects and groups have suffered persecution under the heresy laws but a few examples are of interest here as they appertain to our feline friend.

The first of the 'heretic' sects which was to feel the icy hand of persecution was that of the Gnostic Mani. This Babylonian prince preached dualism, while acknowledging the teachings of Zoroaster, Buddha and Jesus. St. Augustine as a young man was attracted to the religion until it was suppressed by Church and State alike in the early part of the seventh century.

The Manicheans were accused of continually placating the Devil in the form of a black cat. Five hundred years later Europe saw the rise of the Inquisition, founded in 1233 by Pope Gregory IX to root out heresy. At first punishment was a fine or the wearing of a yellow cross, stitched to the clothing. But not for long. The Dominican Order of preacher-friars elected to do the work of the Inquisition. The name means Hounds of God.

The Albigenses (so-named after the town in S.W. France from which they came) and their brother sect the Cathars (the Pure Ones) first appeared in about 1140. Both groups taught that Christ was an angel in a spirit-body. He had revealed the true Albigensian creed and had thus become the Saviour of mankind. The Cathars rejected the world and the eating of flesh. The Church first remonstrated with them and finally in 1283, Pope Gregory IX instituted the Inquisition to exterminate them.

The Waldenses were founded at the end of the twelfth century C.E. by Peter Waldo, a Lyonnaise merchant. He drew a large following and his movement began to spread. Waldenses took the word of Christ literally, gave all they had to the poor and became known as the Poor Men of Lyons. Waldo kept enough money to have the Bible translated as literally as possible, thus defying the Church and bringing the wrath of Rome about his ears.

In 1184 C.E. the Waldenses were excommunicated and declared anathema by Pope Lucius III. They dispersed and made frequent pleas to Rome for mercy. To no avail - Pope Gregory IX instructed the Inquisition to hunt them down. Despite thousands of followers being burnt or tortured to death, the sect still survives to this day.

The third 'heretical sect' of interest here are that band of dedicated gentlemen known as the Knights Templar. They were founded in 1188 C.E. by Hugh de Payens of Champagne to protect the pilgrims and highways to the Holy Land.

Two hundred and fifty years later they were dishonoured, disgraced and disbanded, charged by the Church with among other things, 'unnatural acts, and heresy'. In March, 1314, the last Grand Master of the Order, Jacques de Molay died at the stake. He recanted his confession and cursed those who accused his followers. A curse which soon found retribution.

The followers of each of these sects were accused of worshipping the Devil in the form of a black cat. Confessions were obtained under horrendous torture, the victim being prompted in what to say.

It is ironic that the word 'heresy' comes from the Greek word, 'hairesis', meaning 'option' or - 'choice'. The symbol of the black cat as the Devil implies a choice which should not have been made. Some church pulpits and pillars have been found to bear carvings of obese cats, as if glutted with prey. Some authorities believe that these may have been carved by 'heretic' workmen. The association of the cat with heresy continued well into the seventeenth century when witchcraft was also included. A Prior of the period said, 'The heretic can creep secretly where no man seeth him as doth also the cat who can make herself soft and secret'.

The cat was now regarded as an emissary of the Devil - worse was to follow:

A bad outbreak of St. Vitus' Dance, (An infestation of ergot of rye causing muscular spasms and hallucinations) in Metz, in 1344 was blamed on a black cat. Thirteen cats were caught and publicly burned alive. Similarly, the Black Death of 1347-8 swept across Europe reducing the population by three-quarters. The innocent scapegoat was of course, the cat, as the Devil's accomplice. The Lord Mayor of London gave orders for all cats to be destroyed.

By the end of the fifteenth century, Pope Innocent VII ordered the Inquisition to seek out 'Cat Worshippers'.

House cats and their owners were automatically suspect and the only cats relatively safe were barn cats. Even they were accused of keeping watch for the approach of man, warning the devils at work in the barn.

Within the Church itself divisions appeared. The Protestant movement challenged Catholic orthodoxy. Both factions accused each other of heresy, showing neither mercy nor respect.

On the coronation day of Queen Elizabeth I, a wicker effigy of the Pope was stuffed full of live cats and publicly burnt.

Catholics took a cat, shaved it's poor little head into a tonsure, dressed it in vestments imitating a Protestant Friar then tortured it to death. The common victim in these acts of intolerance and cruelty is, of course, the poor cat.

This persecution of cats was to last for another 450 years.

The Hounds of God were unleashed - now began the Dark Night of the Cat...........

CHAPTER 11

THE DARK NIGHT OF THE CAT

The urge to control Nature by magical means is as old as man himself. Power is a potent wine and taken to excess is a lethal brew. It is no respecter of persons, from the poorest crone to the highest noble in the land, all have succumbed to the temptation of the possibility of gaining power over one's fellows.

From the time of the Plantagenet kings (who were said to have witch-blood), interest in the arts magical became a serious occupation. Alchemy, astrology, demonology, necromancy, witchcraft and divination of all kinds both fascinated and terrified. Secular law forbade it, priests and bishops railed against it from pulpit and palace. All to no avail.

Many magicians were of the nobility, having the benefit of a good education, wealth and contact with other cultures through travel. An upsurge in the quest for knowledge swept through Europe and man questioned the established order. Men such as Galileo fell foul of the Inquisition by declaring that the earth moved around the sun in contrary to orthodox belief. He was accused of heresy, but managed to extricate himself.

Although there is a difference in magical practice between the magician and the witch, both would use anything from nature to achieve their ends and both made use of the cat.

Ritual (or Ceremonial) magicians, by calling themselves astrologers, escaped trouble. The Church frowned, but it was not illegal. Neither did the magician keep a familiar, though this did not save the cat from being used in some horrendous rituals.

Magicians were (nominally) Christians who invoked the protection of the Almighty, in the presence of demons who would destroy them, body, mind and soul, given the chance. Once summoned, the entity would be bribed through sacrifice or forced by the will of the magician to do his bidding. Elaborate and often costly preparations had to be made which focused the raging, intoxicating energy raised in the performance of deeds which could be cruel, perverted and disgusting. Some rites carried out by magicians were enough to raise the hairs on the head of any beldame convicted of witchcraft.

Necromancy was a ritual wherein the magician raised the spirit of the deceased for information As a symbol of chthonic power and the Devil, the cat was doubly useful. One grimoire from Germany gives instructions to write an inscription around the circle, using the blood of a 'mouser' on linen.

In 1323, several people, including one or two churchmen were brought to trial in France charged with necromancy. The circle they cast for the purpose was made from lengths of catskin. Second sight was useful, if not necessary. The harmless way to acquire it is to ensure that you grow from early childhood with a tortoiseshell cat. This does, admittedly depend on the foresight of one's parents. Failing this, if you didn't have the gift naturally, then it could be stolen - from a cat.

Instruction from a fourteenth century manuscript in the collection of the Bodleian Library, Cambridge. is as follows:

> 'So that you may see what others cannot see, mix the bile of a male cat with the fat of a white hen and anoint your eyes with it. You will see what others cannot see'

The Jewish *Talmud* offers this method:

> 'Find and burn the placenta of the first litter of a black cat (which must have been one of it's mother's first litter). Beat it to a powder and rub into the eyes'.

Another method was to blackmail or bribe demons, devils or ancient divinities by torturing their sacred animal.

Up until the end of the eighteenth century, a ritual was practised in parts of Scotland which was surely one of the most horrific ever devised by man: the Taigheirm The word itself means 'the cry of cats' which may convey to you some of the horror: I have deliberately left out details. One such ceremony was held in the middle of the seventeenth century by two men, Allan and Lachlain Maclean, on the Isle of Mull. Allan outlived Lachlain. At Allan's burial, some could see Lachlain's ghost waiting, surrounded by black cats. Visitors to the island may still see the site of the last Taigheirm.

Witchcraft

*'Why should Bridget's cat be worried? Why to be sure
she's black and an imp of darkness.'*

H. Coleridge: Essays (1851)

The witch used the magical wisdom of her forebears. As
often as not, she was illiterate, but it must not be supposed
that witchcraft was the provenance of the peasantry alone.
King William Rufus was overtly pagan and many nobles
had witch-blood coursing through their veins.

In 1441, Eleanor Cobham, Duchess of Gloucester was
charged with using witchcraft to bring about the death of
King Henry VI. Apart from the heresy and witchcraft
accusation, any attempt to bring about the demise of the
monarch was High Treason and carried the death penalty.

Eleanor was the wife of the king's uncle and it may have
been her position that finally saved her life. Her
accomplices suffered the extreme penalty. Queen Elizabeth
Woodville, wife of Edward IV was said (with the help of her
mother), to have invoked the Goddess as Melusine to bring
about her marriage to the young king.

Like all persecutions, the Witchcraft mania of the sixteenth
and seventeenth centuries was the outward expression of a
malaise of society. The witch (and the cat) were the
scapegoats who bore the blame. During that time,
thousands of men and women lost their lives through
suspicion, spiteful gossip or jealousy.

Witchcraft differs from the practice of ritual magic in being
'earthy'. It needs no elaborate equipment, nor the ability to
read Latin, Greek or Hebrew. The witch knows the ways of

The 'Popular' idea of a Witch

nature and respects elemental spirits (which are not demons).

Traditionally meetings are held outside and joyful worship offered the ancient pagan gods. It was this last aspect which drew the attention of the Inquisition. Gods of the Old Religion are ever the Devils of the New. Therefore, was not the witch a heretic, along with the Cathars and Waldenses? All worshipped the Devil. And did not the Devil appear in the form of a black cat?

In the year 1485 C.E. the *'Malleus Maleficarum'* was published which superseded the embarrassingly humane document known as the 'Canon Episcopi' which had been the official Church ruling on the practice of witchcraft.

> *'...some wicked women perverted by the devil, seduced by illusions and phantasms of demons, believe and profess themselves, in the hours of night, to ride upon certain beasts with Diana the goddess of pagans, and an innumerable multitude of women and in the silence of the dead of night ...... to obey her commands as of their mistress, and to be summoned to her service on certain nights. Wherefore the priests...should preach....that such phantasms are imposed upon the minds of infidels and not by the divine but by the malignant spirit.'*

Canon Episcopi. 10th. century C.E.

By the standards of what was to follow, this document was reasonable. It contains three interesting statements:

1. The deity worshipped is Diana, not Satan.

2. Witchcraft is heresy, not black magic.

141

3. The women are suffering from hallucinations and seduced into belief by evil spirits. Echoing the gullibility of woman as first perceived in the Garden of Eden.

It has been argued that confessions obtained at the trials made no mention of the pagan Goddess of the Craft. There are two possible explanations for this: The first being that the Church could not take the risk of admitting a female deity to be powerful. Secondly, the Lady was indeed present, but in a lesser capacity to the (male) Devil and in the form of Diana's cat.

In this respect, a Scottish sorcerer let 'the cat out of the bag'. The man was seen clambering over hedges, chasing cats. This drew suspicion and he was arrested. At his trial he admitted that 'Satan needed all the cats he could get because, without their help he was unable to raise storms and wreck ships'. This implies that Diana, imminent in the cat, was a force to be reckoned with; a point which would not have passed unnoticed by the judges, whose terms of reference were that a witch's power came only through the (male) Devil. Women were considered unable to handle power, they were only instruments. To think otherwise would be to demolish the myth of Eve who was portrayed as being too simple-minded for her own good and in need of guidance and protection.

The *Malleus Maleficarum*, disposed of Diana, substituting Satan as the witches' God. As archetype of evil, Satan's (acquired) cloven feet and horns implicated the pagan Horned Gods also. In addition, Satan had the credibility of being mentioned in the Bible. This effectually by-passed paganism and became seen as a direct assault on the Christian religion. Vestiges still remained: accusations of blight and storm were common which are lunar by association. Shakespeare knew of the pagan connection as he mentions Diana and Hecate in his work, as does Thomas Middleton, in his play, *'The Witch'*.

'A witch; and one so strong she could control the moon - make ebbs and flows'.

Shakespeare: *The Tempest.*

After the publication of the *Malleus Maleficarum*, the Church practised what can only be described as 'selective Christianity'. There was a great deal of emphasis on Biblical passages such as: 'Thou shalt have no other God before Me' and 'Thou shalt not suffer a witch to live'. (This last suffers from the mistranslation of the term 'witch'. The correct word should have been 'poisoner'). There was scant mention of mercy, as in *'Blessed are the merciful...'* or *'Let him that is without sin cast the first stone'*. The scene was set for the holocaust to come.

In an age when household pets were unfamiliar (pardon the pun), any lonely soul who had taken a small animal or bird for company aroused suspicion. There are more records of familiars being in feline form than any other animal. Incidentally, familiar cats were not always black. In Shakespeare's 'Macbeth' the cat was brindled or tabby.

'Thrice the brinded cat hath mewed'.

In return for doing her bidding, the witch was alleged to reward it by giving it a drop of her blood or milk, securing the psychic bond between them.

The familiar warned of psychic presences, aided in divination (often by spirit possession), and carried a magical influence. In the early part of the seventeenth century, Joan and Margaret Flower were hanged for witchcraft in Lincoln. They had wreaked revenge on Margaret's former employers, the Earl and Countess of Rutland. They stole a glove belonging to the Earl's son. This they rubbed on their familiar a cat called Rutterkin, dipped the glove into boiling water, pricked with a pin and buried it. The child died. The women were finally caught. We do not know what happened to the cat - if it had been caught, it would have suffered the same end.

At the age of twelve, Elizabeth Francis took up witchcraft and was given a white spotted cat, called Sathan by her grandmother, Mother Eve. Sathan spoke to her in 'a strange hollow voice' and remained her companion 'for many years'. She passed Sathan to Agnes Waterhouse, who kept him for nine years.

Jennet Dibble of Yorkshire who was tried in the seventeenth century, claimed to have as familiar a black cat called Gibbe, which 'hath attended her now above 40 years'. The cats' longevity is amazing.

Although some familiars were caught and killed, many seemed to vanish when their owners were arrested. It was the complaint of many that 'her spirit hath left her and she never saw him again'.

Raising storms and causing wrecks was a frequent accusation against witches: As early as the seventh century storm-raising was forbidden by Church law and Charlemagne pronounced the death penalty for those who 'disturbed the air and excited tempests'.

At the beginning of the seventeenth century, Agnes Sampson and her coven tried to drown King James I and his bride, Anne of Denmark. They christened a black cat, tied it to part of a corpse and threw it into the sea. The attempt failed, despite a storm which blew up, wrecking a ship nearby. Seafarers to this day still believe that drowning a cat at sea can unleash storms.

Witches were notorious for turning themselves into cats. This is a direct link with the pagan Goddesses who were shape-shifters. A Hungarian tradition holds that cats automatically become witches between the ages of seven and twelve years if this is not prevented by making a cruciform incision in their skin at birth.

The two Goddesses mentioned by Shakespeare, Diana and Hecate both took cat form. Many witches attested at their trials that they favoured turning themselves into cats; the other popular animal form was a hare.

At the trial of Anne Baites in 1673 at Allansford, a witness claimed that Baites 'went into the form of several animals, the pursuer and the pursued'. The song, 'The Coal Black Smith' records this, ending with a mouse and a cat.

Isobel Gowdie, who gave much information to her accusers, gave a detailed explanation of how she transformed herself into a cat: Repeat three times

> 'I shall goe intill ane catt,
> With sorrow, and sych, and a blak shott;
> And I sall goe in the Divellis nam,
> Ay quhill I com hom againe'.

The expression of the last line, 'hom againe' means until she returned to her human form. To achieve this, the following was recited:

'Catt, catt, God send thee a blak shott.
I am in a cattis liknes just now,
Bot I sal be in a womanis liknes ewin now.
Catt, catt, God send thee a blak shott.

Members of Isobel Gowdie's coven changed not only themselves, but each other into cat form. It relied on one witch already being transformed who would say to another, 'The Devil speed thee, go thou with me.' It is possible that hypnosis may have been the key, with a word which acted as a 'trigger' for another (already primed), to believe him/herself to become a cat. This was mentioned in the Canon Episcopi. The other possibility is that the witches were able to turn themselves into cats or shift their consciousness into the body of a cat. This is not impossible.

Another notorious witch, one Isobel Grierson, was accused of changing herself into a cat and breaking into the home of Adam Clark, accompanied by other cats and the Devil himself. She was burnt to death in 1607. One German witch used her shape-shifting abilities to escape from execution. She was sentenced to die by burning: as the flames and smoke rose into the air, there was a loud cry and a black cat jumped from the fire and escaped.

Witches who had taken on cat-form frequently gave themselves away by chattering loudly in human voices. Had they remained silent or paid their respects to the moon in the vocal way that cats do, they may have escaped with nothing more than a boot or bucket of water thrown over them. However, there are several testimonies:

In the year 1718, William Montgomery of Caithness was awoken by chattering outside his window. All he could see were cats. He set about them with his hatchet, killing two and wounding others. The following day, two old women were found dead in their beds and another had a serious wound on her leg for which she had no explanation.

Scott, in his *'Demonology'* records that:

> *'A certain carpenter...was so infested with cats which, as his maid-servant reported, 'spoke among themselves' that...betwixt knife, dirk and broadsword...he made such a dispersion that they were quiet for a night. In the consequences of his blows, two witches were said to have died.'*

Scottish witches were very fond of the cat form and the witches of Mull were particularly adept at it. They sank a Spanish ship with the help of their leader, who appeared on the masthead as a gigantic black cat.

Jane Wenham has the distinction of being the last person to be tried for witchcraft in England. In 1712, she was accused of witchcraft by a neighbour and complained to the authorities. A clergyman dismissed the accusation and Jane was offered compensation. This she refused, but was later accused of turning herself into a cat to frighten a servant girl. It is interesting that the attitude of those in authority was lenient whereas folk memory still lived on.

Folk-memory did indeed live on: in Kidderminster, Worcs. lived Betty Swan during the nineteenth century. Betty was a white witch who was an excellent healer and could be relied upon to find lost property. One day, a large black cat wandered into the village and went to Betty's door scratching at it until she let it in. The cat was seen from time to time but on the fourth day, the door remained closed and no smoke came from the chimney. When neighbours broke in, the cat shot up the chimney and all that remained of Betty were ashes on the floor.

At the end of the nineteenth century, the Basques still claimed that witches still turned themselves into cats.

It must not be assumed that all Churchmen were ailurophobes. Many loved their cats, and despaired at the mania going on outside their palace walls.

Cardinal Wolsey, the faithful adviser of King Henry VIII could not bear to be parted from his tabby cat. It even accompanied him when he said Mass in Westminster Cathedral.

Pope Pius IX had a cat which would sit opposite him at meals, 'silent and respectful'. This cat sat on the Holy Father's knee while he gave audiences.

Pope Leo XII loved his cat Micetto, who was born in the Vatican. Upon his death, Micetto was cared for by Chateaubriand, who adored cats.

Cardinal Richelieu, the seventeenth century statesman who virtually ruled France was a good friend to cats: he set aside a room in his palace for them. He left money for his cats to live in comfort after his death. His Eminence had a wry sense of humour as one of his cats was called Lucifer.

With the Act of 1736 abolishing the witchcraft laws, things eased gradually for the cat. I say gradually because it is easier to change the law than the mind of a human being with attitude.

During the eighteenth century, cats became not just pets, but fashionable pets once more. A plague of brown rats, more dangerous to health than their black relatives were dealt with by puss, securing a place for the cat in man's home.

The Victorian era saw even greater popularity: the Queen herself had two blue Persian cats, one of them called Heather. When Queen Victoria's first daughter was born, the Queen referred to her in the same affectionate term as the ancient Egyptians did their little girls: the Queen called her, 'Pussy'. The wheel had come full circle.

CHAPTER 12

THE CAT IN FABLE

Fables and fairy stories are found in every culture. They were originally used to teach and explain morality and good citizenship to the young.

Whatever their age or origin, these tales still have the power to entrance children of all ages. They speak to us of discovery and innocence, of a time when the world was truly wonderful and everything was possible. What adult does not secretly enjoy a pantomime as much as the children do?

Animal heroes (and heroines) are the focus of many of our favourite stories and pantomimes. They teach us faith and perseverance, kindness and unselfishness, cruelty and guile in a way which would lose much of it's impact if the hero were a human. Why? Because an animal archetype speaks to our inner selves. We automatically associate them with a quality, for example, the owl with wisdom, the lion with royalty, the dog with faithfulness and the cat with....what? The cat is always a mystery. Like a human character the cat has a choice of action. We wait to see 'which way the cat will jump', for good or ill. It is this unpredictability which makes us sit up and accept instruction and advice from a source which we would normally not expect to find it. What about Puss in Boots and Dick Whittington?

As the cat-nature holds within itself extremes of character, the fables use this to illustrate the same trait within man - only more so.

Stories in which the cat is a dominant character generally fall into two types: the cat which is selfish, thoughtless and treats others with disdain; these usually contain warnings of 'leopards don't change their spots' and 'you should have known better' variety. Keep alert and vigilant. A tale by Aesop observes that however much we try to change our image, we are still ourselves underneath:

> *A young man fell in love. Instead of joy, this only brought him despair because the object of his love was a cat. In desperation, he entreated Venus to help him. She took pity on him and changed the cat into a lovely young woman. The pair were married and that night as they lay abed, a mouse crept across the floor. The bride immediately chased it. Venus was angry that the bride should put mice before her husband's love and changed her back into a cat.*

Also from Aesop:

> *'A cat heard of sickness which had broken out in an aviary. Seeing his chance for a free meal, he disguised himself as a doctor and with a medical bag set out. He arrived and offered his services but was detected before he could do further harm.'.*

A similar tale is told in India where:

A cat repented of his wicked ways and went to the Ganges to atone. He did this daily, and very soon other birds and small animals, convinced of his sincerity began to visit him. They only visited him once. While the cat continued to sit by the Ganges.... and live well.

An Italian cautionary tale, warning of pride:

A cockerel wished to achieve his life-long ambition to become Pope. A cat offered to accompany him to Rome. The foolish, vain bird accepted the offer but never arrived because the cat ate him.

La Fontaine (1621-1695) wrote many excellent tales, among them the wiles of a cat called Rodilard:

Rodilard was the scourge of all mice. They knew him well and always kept out of his way. Rodilard therefore began to get very hungry. His hunger sharpened his wits and he thought of a plan. Taking some rope, he tied himself upside down from a hook, holding the free end in his paw. There he remained, seemingly dead. After a while, the mice decided that Rodilard had met a well-deserved end and felt bold enough to come and play. They were so confident that they sent word to their friends the rats. All made merry, ignoring Rodilard. He suddenly pulled the rope, jumped down and dealt thoroughly with the rodents. Some managed to escape to holes so Rodilard covered himself with cornmeal and hid in the bran tub, holding his breath until the rodents came to feast. And then...... some people just don't learn, do they?

152

Some tales show it is the cat who is gullible or used by others: this story was told to children in India over three thousand years ago:

A lion lived in a cave where he was greatly troubled by a mouse which nightly came and chewed his mane. He finally went to the nearest town and found a homeless cat, promising to treat it well if it would keep the mouse away.

For a while, all went well. One night, the mouse was hungry and crept from it's hiding place, only to be pounced upon and eaten by the cat.

When the lion discovered that the mouse no longer existed, he threw the cat out of the cave. The cat had to return to the town and live as miserable a life as before.

And:

A monkey and a cat sat before a fire, roasting chestnuts. The monkey carefully arranged the nuts in the ashes and persuaded the cat to pull them out with her paw. As the cat licked her blistered paw, the monkey ate all the nuts. This is the origin of the term 'catspaw'.

Several of these tales reflect the attitude to the cat in earlier times: resourceful, cunning and merciless. In contrast to these, the tales below illustrate how we may prosper if we show kindness or accept advice from an unusual quarter.

Another Italian story:

A woman had many hungry children, but no money to buy food. A faery appeared and told her that if she were to climb a nearby mountain, she would find a palace inhabited by cats who may give her alms. She found the palace and was admitted by a kitten. She looked round and was horrified by the mess and clutter. Forgetting her purpose, she immediately began to tidy, clean and put into good order. The kitten returned and she was shown into the king's presence. He asked what she wanted and she explained her situation. He rang a golden bell and asked how the woman had spent her time whilst waiting. On hearing of her help, the king ordered that her apron should be filled with as many gold coins as she could carry.

This story is similar to the legend of St. Yves who gives alms to the poor while a cat sits at his side.

Puss In Boots

A miller had three sons. On his deathbed he left the mill to the eldest, his ass to the next and his cat to the youngest.

At first the youngest son was disappointed in his legacy, but the cat spoke to him, asking for a pair of boots and a sack. With those he promised to make the lad's fortune.

The lad did as requested and the cat, resplendent in his boots took the sack to a rabbit warren, sprinkled it with corn and lay down as if asleep. Soon a rabbit crept out of the hole and began to eat the corn.

Puss leapt up, killed the rabbit, put it in the sack and made for the king's palace.

At the palace he presented the rabbit as a gift from his master, 'the Marquis of Carabas', which was gratefully accepted.

The following day he took a gift of two pheasants to the king, with the same result.. The king decided to pay a visit to the marquis and calling his daughter they set out in the royal coach.

The cat hastened to his master and told him to go and bathe in the river at a spot which he would show. The son did so, and the cat hid his poor clothes under a stone.

As the king's coach drew near, the cat ran before it, asking aid for his master, the Marquis of Carabas, who has been bathing and robbed of his clothes. The king immediately sent for some of the finest from his palace for the young man and offered him a place in the coach.

The cat ran before the coach to a field where peasants were cutting the corn. Calling them, the cat warned them that if they did not tell the king that the fields belonged to the Marquis of Carabas, ill fortune would befall them.

As the coach passed, the king called a peasant and asked the owner of such fine land. The peasant answered as instructed and the coach moved on. The king very impressed with the now bewildered man who sat before him.

The cat ran again before the coach through a forest to a magnificent palace which belonged to a cruel ogre, the real owner of the lands so admired by the king.

The cat was admitted to the ogre's presence and at once regaled him with tales of hearsay about the ogre's skill with magic. The ogre, proud, turned himself into a lion. The cat was unimpressed. Anyone can make themselves look bigger than they are. What about something smaller? What about a mouse? This the ogre immediately did and was eaten by the cat.

By this time the king's coach was heard in the courtyard below and the cat ran to the door to receive them.

When all were seated in the great hall, the cat gave orders for a sumptuous feast to be prepared. By this time, the miller's youngest son was speechless with wonder. The king took this for shyness because of the lad's obvious attraction to the princess, and hers to him. The king gave permission for them to marry. They did so in great joy. The cat attended in a new pair of boots made from crimson leather, set with diamonds.

The moral here is faith and trust. The only casualty of the story was the evil ogre, who got all he deserved anyway.

The White Cat

This French tale again involves the youngest of three sons and his father's inheritance: this time the father is the king and the inheritance the crown. The three tasks were to find the most intelligent small dog, to find a length of material which would pass through the eye of a needle. The third was to find the most beautiful woman in the world.

The young son sets off hopefully and comes to a palace where he falls in love with a beautiful white cat. The boy stays with her for a year and she helps him to succeed over his brothers with the first task. With the second task, the boy once again seeks her help. He stays another year and returns with his contribution, wrapped, as he hoped in a walnut shell. Opening the shell in front of the assembled court, he finds within a hazel nut shell, inside that a cherry stone and in that, a millet seed. At this point, he falters, believing himself deceived. He receives a scratch on his hand. The material is within the millet seed and he again wins.

With the third task, he returns to the White Cat. Before leaving for his father's palace at the appointed time, the Cat tells him to cut off her head and tail. He by now loves her dearly and begs to be excused from this task. She insists. He complies and as he throws the head and tail into the fire, she turns into a beautiful princess. Once again he succeeds and eventually wins the throne and his bride.

Cinderella

Cinderella is a story told in many countries. The oldest version comes to us from Italy and is called, *'La Gatta Cenerentola'* - *'The Cinderella Cat'*. The version of the story we are familiar with is that of the French writer, Perrault.

Both versions however, focus the story on a beautiful young virgin who sits at the hearth and is badly used by her family. One day, she is visited by her fairy-godmother who

Dick Whittington's Cat on a Milestone, Highgate Hill

transforms her rags and sends her to the ball. She finally marries the king's son.

Catskin

This is an English story, which has many parallels to Cinderella. A young girl sits by the hearth, with a catskin round her shoulders. She slaves away for an ungrateful family, but manages to attend the ball given by the king. She finally marries a nobleman.

In versions of this tale from Brittany and Denmark, the skin is given her by a cat who begs for milk at the door. The girl always gives, despite being thrashed for doing so. The cat is transformed into a prince.

Alternatively, in an Irish version the godmother is a cat. In these tales the cat comes to the aid of the heroine. The mice, which are usually destructive are put to good use pulling the pumpkin coach.

Both mice and pumpkins are lunar objects, again signifying transformation. Like the Whit Cat, the true self was already immanent inside the young girl, released by the power of love.

Dick Whittington

Finally, the story of a man who actually lived: Dick Whittington. The story concerns a poor lad who journeyed to London to make his fortune. On the way, he meets a starving cat, feeds it and it becomes his companion. He finds work as a scullery-boy and the cat keeps down the mice which over-ran the kitchen. One day, he puts his cat on the master's boat to be sold, that he may better himself. The cat is bought by the king of a country where cats were unknown and mice a great problem.

Dick meanwhile decided to return home, having neither money nor friend. In the tolling of the bells he hears them call him to return, which he does. His master's ship returns home with a fortune for the boy from the sale of his cat to a grateful monarch. He is an historical character who was indeed mayor of London three times.

In latter years, the 'cat' in the story has been thought to be the name for the type of vessel which put to sea. If so, the (feline) cat would be sadly missed. There is a point in favour of this change; the story would be free of the unfortunate message that a man once sold his only friend in the world for gold. I wonder whether it ever bothered his conscience? Perhaps the sacrifice of the cat was not in vain: Whittington was certainly a good man and provided libraries, built alms-houses for the poor, and restored St. Bartholomew's Hospital. He died in 1423.

These last three tales tell us to sacrifice what we are and what we have for what we may become. The virgins who sat at the hearth were echoes of the virgin priestesses of Vesta. Vesta guarded the fires of home and the sacred flame of Rome also. The cat was also regarded as the protector of the hearth by the Romans, hence the two together.

These stories also show current attitudes to the cat. At the time of writing, since the eighteenth century, the cat had once again become a popular pet.

Descriptions and illustrations show the cat wearing clothes: it has become anthropomorphised to an amazing degree. The cat can do no wrong.

CHAPTER 13

CURIOUS CATS

The cat world has it's share of the odd and the unusual. Some of the cats in this section are mythical, others are real cats but with - a difference.

Fabulous beasts are mainly the inventions of mankind's imagination. Some are composite animals, made from two or more species. They appear as heraldic emblems, in mythology as monsters and as characters in works of fiction.

Whether fact or fiction, many are believed in. Classical writers list many which are now seen to be the result of hearsay. Medieval bestiaries attempted to portray wild animals in keeping more with the qualities which they represented rather than their accurate physical forms.

The process is continuing too, listed below are several examples which have come into modern folklore.

Cactus Cat

This strange being is to be found in an area between north and central America. The coat was tough and thorny and the ears ended in long spines. On the legs above the front feet, the bones were like knife-blades. The tail was branched. The cactus cat would use the 'knife-bones' to hack at the giant cactus stems. The resulting sap flowed out for several days. The cat would return and by this time, the sap had become a fermented, sticky mess. This sap the cat would drink until thoroughly tipsy, then it would then rush away, rasping it's forelegs together and uttering horrible shrieks.

Cat-A-Mountain

An animal well-known in medieval heraldry. Writers of the period used the term for any large cat. The explorer, Marco Polo claims to have seen one. He describes it as large as a leopard with a wide mouth and keen eyesight. The body was covered in thin skin which formed 'wings' when the animal flew from tree to tree. This may easily be a flying squirrel or bat, embellished with a long journey and constant telling.

Ccoa

A cat-spirit which plagued the Quechua Indians of Peru. It was about two feet in length with a one foot long tail. It had a very large head, with eyes and ears which constantly poured hail. The coat had horizontal stripes.

Cheshire Cat

The famous grinning cat from Lewis Carroll's *'Alice in Wonderland'*. This cat had very long claws and teeth. It was prone to disappearing gradually, the last part of it to vanish being its smile.

The expression, 'to grin like a Cheshire cat' goes back to the seventeenth century. The reason for it is not known with any certainty. It may be a reminder of the Cheshire cheeses which were sold with a cat's face moulded on them, similar to those sold in bath during the last century.

Divis

A creature of Persian myth. A cat-headed man with horns and hooves. Possibly a being 'demonised' from an earlier religion.

Gib-Cat

Unlike the Cheshire cat, this unfortunate is renowned for his melancholic expression. The expression Gib-cat or Gilbert, dates back to 1843. It is the name given to 'doctored' tom-cats who thereafter wear an unhappy expression.

Guirivulu

A monster which was cat-like in form with a tail ending in a large claw. This creature attacked bathers and boatmen, changing into a serpent as it crushed them.

Para

A Scandinavian feline spirit, found mostly in Finland and Sweden (where it is known as a Bjara). In Lapland it was the cream cat, 'Smierragatto'. This spirit would collect dairy produce for the owner.

Sea-Cat

Reported by St. Brendan on one of his voyages. He was warned of the beast whilst visiting an unknown island. It was said to be large, with long teeth and growing bigger every day from the quantity of fish it consumed. The eyes were like 'glass'. This is a very good description of one of the seal family: they have whiskers, cat-like ears and 'glass-like' eyes.

Silver Cat

An unfriendly cat from the north American pine-woods. Resembling a cat, the eyes were red, vertical slits. The tail was long ending in a hard knob, which was smooth on one side and spiked on the other.

Lumberjacks were this creatures particular delicacy: it would wait on an overhead branch, knock the man down with the smooth side and lift him up with the spike.

Splinter Cat

An American creature which split trees by flying at them and pounding the trunk with it's forehead. The creature did this in order to get at the bees and racoons which were it's diet. The resulting damage looked as if the tree had suffered from a storm.

The next section contains information on cats which have actually lived (and thrived). They were winged cats, and for the disbelieving there is photographic evidence. The 'wings' were appendages which grew from just behind the shoulder, covered in fur.

Winged Cats

The earliest record of a winged cat comes from Somerset at the close of the last century. A picture of it appeared in the 'Strand' magazine, November, 1899. Since that time, another was recorded in the Leeds Workhouse. This unfortunate animal ended up in a side-show in a fairground. It was stuffed after it's death.

Two more cats were recorded during the nineteen thirties. It appeared that although the wings could not be used to fly, they did enable the cat to jump a greater distance than would otherwise have been possible.

Cat-Headed Men

It was Mark Twain who observed that if man could be crossed with the cat, the result would be an improvement to man but a backward step for the cat. From which you may have guessed that Mr. Twain was a great cat-lover.

The idea of crossing men with animals goes way back to the dawn of time. Gods and Goddesses have been depicted as being part animal, but to emphasise a particular attribute or facet of their personality. Bastet is one such goddess who was never represented as a full woman, but has been as a full cat.

A few examples of Man crossed with Animal spring to mind: Chiron the Centaur who had the torso of a man and the body of a horse, the Minotaur who had the body of a man and the head of a bull, mermen, with the body of a man and from the waist downwards, the tail of a fish.

Like the cat itself, cat-men are elusive but there are two examples:

The first is from Celtic mythology. Cairbre Cinn-Cait, who usurped the Irish throne from the Milesians. Cairbre, like the fierce, black Celtic cat was a cruel man. Whether he wore a cat-skin over his head or actually had the features of a cat cannot be known for sure. Tradition points to the latter as he killed all his sons who were born with similar features.

A Persian king called Hormus was held under siege in his capital by rebel forces. He was outnumbered and called for an adviser. He was told that he could defeat the rebels very quickly if he could enlist the services of a cat-faced man. The king sent soldiers out at night under cover of darkness to find such a man.

Eventually such a man was found who was a mountaineer. The king immediately put him in charge of the army and such was his leadership that with an army of only 12,000 men, he defeated the opposing army of 300,000 men.

There is an interesting African tale concerning the fate of a young wife whose tribe claimed descent from a cat.

A young woman whose name was Titishana had recently married and was to leave for her husband's village. As she was permitted to take an animal with her, she chose the totem animal, the cat. Her parents tried to dissuade her, but she insisted.

At first all went well, but before long, the cat started to take the husband's rattle and dance with it. One night the husband awoke and killed the cat. Titishana fainted. When she regained consciousness, she asked her husband to cover the cat. They returned the dead cat to the girl's tribe and all who looked at it dropped dead. Very soon the entire village had died. So entwined were the lives of the people and the cat. The husband had lost all, including his wife and her dowry - there was nobody left alive to reclaim it from.

CHAPTER 14

THE CAT AND ASTROLOGY

Stand up those of you who said, 'The only cat in astrology is Leo!' Yes, but Leo is a lion, a cousin to our small friend - and there are a few surprises with Leo, too. The little cat is there in many guises, subtle and enigmatic, true as always to itself. The archetypal cat is found, in varying degrees in each sign of our western zodiac.

Sometimes the ruler of a sign is the link, such as the Sun, Moon and Venus. Sometimes the connection is through shared attributes of the sign's ruler with other deities. More subtle are those signs with no obvious connection. But all are valid, all express some aspect of the essence of cat-ness.

Let us first define astrology, how it works, what it does and how it is used. Many people equate astrology with their 'stars' in the national press. Unfortunately, the predictions given each morning centre on one aspect of the whole (the Sun sign) which gives a rather distorted result. Because of this, they fall short of accuracy.

Astrology should be carried out on a personal basis: there is only one you, born at a particular time and place. (Even twins differ in time of birth).

Astrology is a tool for understanding yourself, what influences make you tick. A birth-chart shows your strengths and weaknesses, relative to each other. The Mystery Cults of the ancient world had one instruction: *'Man, Know Thyself'*. Astrology helps us to do that. Foretelling the future, choosing whether a time is 'good' or 'bad' to start a project, the comparison of charts of people who are entering into a marriage/business partnership are all useful side-lines, and can be surprisingly accurate.

How does it work? Just as all life is one, so is the Universe. Each movement influences the whole in a manner which our inadequate senses cannot yet perceive. However, by studying those movements which can be measured, we can use this to examine the influences on our lives Astrology does not compel. We all have free-will and choice of action as the cat symbolises. Using it wisely is another matter.

Definitions of some terms may be useful to those not familiar with them.

Cardinal: Outgoing, capable of taking responsibility. Mark the change of season by the Equinoxes and Solstices. These occur as the sun moves into a cardinal sign.

Fixed: Static, defends the status quo and is resistant to change. The four Celtic festivals of Beltane, Lammas, Samhain and Imbolc fall in fixed signs.

Mutable: Flexible, changeable, bends with the wind.

Earth: Solid, dependable, practical, tactile, 'sensual' as in gratification of the senses.

Fire: Inspiration, activity, enthusiasm.

Air: The mind and intellect. Communicative.

Water: Emotion. Sensitivity, fluidity.

Aries the Ram:

Ruler: Mars. Cardinal Fire.

The first sign of the zodiac because the Sun enters the sign at the Vernal Equinox and it was therefore the first day of the Roman New Year.

The rulership of Mars may not at first seem obvious, but he was the god of Springtime (as well as war). It is in this context that he shares with Osiris, as god of the growing corn. The soul of Osiris was also known as the Ram (not Goat) of Mendes. Osiris often takes the form of a cat in his aspect as god of growing corn. As a chthonic deity he is also responsible for the resting time of the seed in the Underworld; a duty he shares with Hades/Pluto. More has been said about Osiris and the cat in earlier chapters. The sign of Aries contains in itself all the activity and energy for growth and renewal.

Mars is also the god of war. Cats have been used in war situations by many cultures. Persian soldiers held cats before them to prevent attack by the Egyptians who surrendered. The soldiers from ancient Thailand took their cats with them when on sentry duty. Perched on the man's shoulder, the cat would yell at the sight of a stranger in the distance. The goddesses of music and dance Bastet and Hathor, were also capable of ferocity. Their emblem, the sistrum was used as much for dance as for summoning the troops. Nothing fights as fiercely as two cats.

Taurus the Bull:

Ruler: Venus. Fixed Earth.

Venus, goddess of love and sexual pleasure also equates with Greek Aphrodite, Egyptian Bastet and Norse Freya. Freya rides in a chariot drawn by two cats. Bowls of milk were left outside Scandinavian homes for Freya's cats to refresh themselves, hoping that for this kindness, the goddess would bless their fields and reward with an abundant harvest. The Celtic festival of Beltaine celebrating the beginning of summer comes under this sign.

Venus has rulership over spring, fertility, gardens, herbs, perfumes, flowers and music. She also has dominion over two signs in our western zodiac. Taurus and Libra. The same attributes are present in each sign, but with different emphasis. The first, Taurus, is earthy, loving sensation and feeling. In this sign the influence of Venus works through a female medium. The Taurean Venus delights in prosperity: be it money or the vegetable garden. Luxury, pleasure and comfort are her delight and she will give herself for the sheer pleasure of giving and receiving love.

Prostitution comes under the influence of Venus. In Rome, on the 23rd and 25th April, prostitutes kept their holy days at the temple of Venus just outside the city. Late April and early May were holidays given over to sexual licence. The festival of Bastet took place at this time, also. At one time, young women would give themselves in the temples. As such, they were holy and instruments of the goddess. In modern times, prostitution has a less worthy implication, and brothels are often called 'cathouses'.

The Roman dictator, Cornelius Sulla added *'Felix'* to his name, which he translated from the Greek, *'Epaphriditos'*, meaning *'Aphrodite's darling'*.

This Venus also possesses: Once in love, she will cling to her beloved with claws if necessary.

Taurus rules music, dancing and with rulership over the throat, therefore singing too. The cat's cry has 63 notes and anyone who has lain awake in the wee small hours listening to their nocturnal chorus will know how expressively these can be used.

Bastet and Hathor were both associated with music. Hathor was the 'Lady of Music and Mistress of Song' and she was described as 'Merry as Bastet'. The instrument common to both of them was the sistrum, a form of rattle consisting of a loop with four loose rods through it. Sistra have been found with figures of cats either on top of the loop or above the handle. Most of them have an engraving of Hathor.

The instrument found its way to Rome with the worship of Isis. From Portici paintings were found showing a priest of Isis and a woman rattling sistra before a cat, itself seated on a large sistrum. Another (unlikely) divinity associated with Bast was Bes, who appears as a nude dwarf. He rules music, dance and women in childbirth. A temple carving shows Bes standing at the foot of a pillar on top of which is a cat's head.

Gemini the Twins:

Ruler Mercury. Mutable Air.

This is the first sign to introduce the symbol of humanity and the concept of mind. The Twins imply two minds making a choice. If identical twins, this sign may also point to a person 'being in two minds'. Ruled by Mercury with his caduceus of twinned serpents symbolising the power of sun and moon, the conscious and unconscious mind. They represent balanced pairs of equal-opposites: male and female, positive and negative, hot and cold, good and bad. In Gemini, the mind is active enough to examine all possibilities before making a choice.

The cat in this sign can be taken to represent the duality of the cat (and human) nature. Bastet-Sekhmet are appropriate here as the dual effect of the sun on our lives: mild and fructifying or searing and destructive. Ours is the conscious choice, the invitation to make a decision for good or ill.

Mercury, the ruler of this sign is also the god of merchants: Dick Whittington made his fortune with the aid of his cat. Japanese shopkeepers put the 'Beckoning Cat' outside their premises to draw customers within. Many Japanese shopkeepers also keep a cat or two on their counters, secured by a collar and chain. The older the cat, the luckier they are considered to be for business. Gemini is the sign not only of duality but duplicity as well: the cat, it must be admitted can be a thief *par excellence*.

A Hungarian tradition states that the best mousers are cats which have been stolen. The 'Hand of Glory', the embalmed hand used by thieves to gain entrance undetected has for one of it's ingredients the ashes of a black cat. Fables

173

abound which show the cat to be up to tricks with the gullible. La Fontaine tells of Rodilard the fraudster who tricked mice and rats to their deaths.

An epic tale from India tells of a 'penitent' cat who fooled other animals into thinking that he had given up his wicked ways only to discover their mistake when they ended up as lunch. Gemini is the sign of youth about to explore the environment in which it lives: small children and kittens epitomise play at it's most endearing. We should all appreciate the benefits of play, whatever our age.

Cancer the Crab:

Ruler the Moon. Cardinal. Water.

The Moon rules water. Our bodies are over 70% water, we begin life in a fluid and until we die, we cannot live for long without water. We express emotion with tears. Water and the Moon are passive. Water needs to be contained, the Moon receives and reflects light. The cat, like the Moon carries the light of the Sun through the darkness. The Moon illuminates the night and our inner selves, we receive 'enlightenment'.

The festival of Midsummer is in the sign of Cancer when the Sun reaches the highest point north of the equator. There is some confusion with the terms 'Solstice' and 'Midsummer'. The solstice is when the sun achieves it's maximum distance north of the equator, giving us the longest day: after that time, the daylength decreases. It is given as a time and can vary between 21st and 22nd June. The day following is Midsummer, often called St. John's Day. Midsummer revelries always included a large bonfire to encourage the sun. Both during pagan times and later, cats were burnt alive in these fires. The solar cat became the fire itself.

The Solstice is important because that day marks the entry of the Sun into the sign of Cancer, described as the 'Sign of the Waters of Life'. Note that the sun is at it's most powerful in Cancer, rather than in it's own sign of Leo. The strongest penetrative rays are needed for fertility. Cancer is the sign governing motherhood and fertility. The result of that union, the child, belongs to the sign of Leo.

Cancer also rules emotional security. Faithless women in both Iceland and, surprisingly, Egypt were tied in a sack with a cat and thrown into water. In Iceland such places were called the drowning pools.

Leo the Lion:

Ruler the Sun. Fixed Fire.

Leo is the majesty of Ra, whose name is still found in words referring to rulership: raja, regal, royal, reign, le roi, regiment. His metal is gold, symbol of the Sun in which the Great Cat loves to bask.

The lion is the 'King of Beasts', so why is Ra not depicted as a lion? The answer is because the lion does not kill venomous snakes and scorpions. The cat does. This applies not only to serpents of the animal world, but serpents as deities. Leo is in stressful relation (aspect) to Scorpio, who has rulership over these.

Leo is the Sun at noon, fixed, moving not at all. The Sun cannot go retrograde (backwards in relation to the movements of the other planets) It can only go forward and beyond the point of noon, loses power. Many kings have fallen because of their inability to either assert themselves (cardinality) or adopt a flexible attitude (mutability). King Charles I was of the latter persuasion. On the day before he was arrested, his little black cat died and the King tearfully observed that his luck had died also.

The Sun in Leo is slightly past his peak performance (in Cancer). The fixicity of fire shows him trying to maintain the status quo. The child's game, the 'cat's cradle' was originally a ritual of sympathetic magic to make a complex net with which to catch the sun and slow it's progress towards winter. The cat's cradle is found even as far north as the Eskimo cultures.

During the course of this sign comes Lammas or Lughnasadh, the Feast of Bread, when sacrifices of either king or sacred animal were made to add strength to that of the waning Sun. The King or animal were considered to be his living representatives, thus holding some of his power. By sacrificing them, 'God-Force' was released to invigorate the Sun. The glyph of Leo is a lion's tail, originally that of a lioness. The lioness (Sekhmet) is far fiercer than her husband and it is she who does most of the hunting. Tails are thought to be imbued with a great deal of magical power, hence the glyph.

Virgo the Virgin:

Ruler Mercury. Mutable Earth

The second earth sign but this time implying movement. This earth is still solid and dependable but allows change. Virgo contains the practicality of earth combined with the need to understand (Mercury). Virgoans are generally

176

analytical folk who take matter apart in an effort to perfect. Thus the grain is ground, winnowed and sifted. During Virgo, the harvest is finally completed and gathered in. In the fields, the cat as Spirit of the Corn would be caught, sacrificed (either symbolically or actually) and returned to the earth for the next harvest. This balances with the opposite sign of self-sacrifice, Pisces.

Virgo is the only feminine figure in our western zodiac. Earth-goddesses Isis, Demeter and even the Virgin Mary have been associated with this sign, and all have a link with the cat. Demeter's symbols are a grain of wheat and a poppy. The grain of wheat is fertility and the poppy tells of the long sleep which follows. One of the attributes of Virgo is health and cleanliness. The Virgo cat protects and cleanses the barns and granaries against damage by rodents.

The Hindu word for cat is translated as 'the cleanser'. In China, the festival of Li-Shou, the god of the gathered harvest takes place near this time and he takes the form of a cat. From a western point of view, Li-Shou is typically Virgoan: he is a practical deity(earth) who reacts to a need (mutable). In earlier days, the fire of Leo burnt the stubble from the fields and the Equinoctial gales scattered the ashes over the bare earth. After this time, night gains on day.

Libra the Scales:

Ruler Venus. Cardinal Air.

Venus rules the sign of Libra. Libra is an air sign and therefore masculine. This Venus is elegant, beautiful and detached. Unlike earthy Taurus, Libran Venus' head always rules her heart. She is similar to the Virgin Goddesses who belong to no man. Here we find the kings' mistresses. Proud and elegant, loving the king (the sun in Leo), but not possessed by him. These women were often married to suitable courtiers, but the marriage was one of name only. Air demands freedom of movement and symbolises intelligence, justice and liberty. The kings' mistresses were often the real power behind the throne, manipulating events both personal and political, having more influence than the queen herself. Like an elegant cat basking in the heat of the sun, king's mistress always knows when it is time to move so as not to be burnt by the sun's rays.

A painting by Edouard Manet entitled *'Olympia'* catches the essence of the Libran Venus. She reclines, naked, on her couch. At her feet sits a little black cat.

Marriage comes under the sign of Libra. The goddess who is patron of fertility finds herself having domain over marriage. Harmonious marriage is bliss. A discordant marriage can be hell. Here is Libran (thinking) Venus in direct opposition to Arian (impulsive)Mars. Venus' cat uses her claws, not to hold but to wound.

Not surprisingly, Libra is also the sign of enemies and rivals. Aphrodite, the Greek counterpart of Venus was known to cause pain to her lovers if they displeased her: One lover had his eyes stung by bees for seeing her naked, another, Pygmalion, fell in love with a statue and Adonis died, to be resurrected each year. Queens who committed adultery were automatically guilty of treason, for which the penalty was death by burning. Treason is an offence against the state, threatening the liberty of the people. The cuckolded husband (Leo) acting as the fiery, solar cat. Queen Anne Boleyn, the beautiful, black-haired queen of

Henry VIII has something very feline about her: her sentence of 'burning' was changed to decapitation.

Liberty is a byword when speaking of cats. Nobody owns a cat, we mislead ourselves if we think we do. The cat has been a symbol of liberty and justice for many centuries. Liberty is always a woman. Statues of the goddess of Liberty show a cat at her feet. Roman legions carried banners with cats signifying defence of their rights and freedom. The Roman goddess of the corn, Ceres, equates with Cat-Demeter of Greece. As provider of bread for the people, Ceres also protected the rights and liberties of the common man. Some priestesses served in both the temples of Ceres and Venus.

Other European countries have also adopted the cat as a symbol of liberty:

Holland chose a cat to place on their ensign in their struggle with the Spanish. The French Republic placed a cat at the side of Liberty. The Republican artist, Prud'hon painted a picture of the French Constitution, now in Dijon. He shows Liberty in a phrygian cap, holding a broken chain and a pike. At her feet is a cat.

The figure of Justice is a woman (She is not Venus, despite her association with the sign of Libra). The Egyptian goddess, Net (who equates with Greek Athene) was a wise counsellor and arbitrator in the struggle between Horus and Set. A sacred cat was kept at her temple in Sais. Isis as regent in Osiris' absence, governed well and fairly. The scales of Ma'at, equated with Bastet are seen in the sigil of Libra. St. Yves, the patron saint of lawyers is shown with a cat.

The Libran cat sits in the Courts of Justice in France at the verdict of a 'Crime Passionel'. Furious Venus. Whereas British Law makes no provision for a 'crime of passion', the French system understands well the violent emotions which erupt from the soul which outraged love causes, leading to loss of self control with tragic results.

Scorpio the Scorpion:

Ruler Mars and Pluto. Fixed Water.

Fixed water exists as ice. The Scorpion is a creature of darkness and secrecy: even it's sting is in the tail and is greater than may be expected for a creature of it's size. The Mayas called the scorpion the 'god of death' and the Egyptians set Mafdet, the cat/lynx headed goddess to control it. Bastet was bitten badly by a scorpion and appealed to Ra for help.

The serpent of darkness comes under this sign, as do serpents who are connected with the halls of the Underworld. The Egyptian Book of the Dead mentions one such being. The Scorpio gaze is riveting and compelling, like the gaze of cat or snake.

Scorpio heralds the beginning of the Celtic winter at Samhain (All Hallows), which was also the beginning of their New Year. Diana rides her cat through the night skies and the Devil in the form of a black cat was believed to preside over the Sabbat.

This is the feast of the dead when the veil is thin between the worlds. This is the time of the sorrowing mother, the crone, who grieves over the loss of her son/brother/husband. Set is the essence of darkness and has been identified with

Apep, which is daily slain by the Solar Cat. There is a tension between Scorpio and Leo in their fixicity: neither giving way to the other.

Set was accused of sexually abusing Osiris: the sexual act comes under Scorpio. If however Set was the original female principle of Creation, then this act was understandable, his/her domain is the parched desert; having the same effect as ice which is water in suspension, denying fruition of that act. Set murdered Osiris during the month of Hathor (November). Osiris then entered the Underworld as the Judge of the dead. This sign is associated with the mystic cycle of transformation: it crosses and penetrates the boundaries of the sexual act and death - the potential and withdrawing of life rather than the process of life itself. Mars is the energy and stimulus for the process, Pluto as chthonic deity of the Underworld, transforms and preserves the energy for later rebirth. With the drawing in of the days, the Scorpio cat sits at the feet of the old woman who contemplates what has gone before and what may be to come: enlightenment is to be found in the dark recesses of our subconscious minds. A time to review the past year and anticipate the next. A time for self-analysis, to take stock before treading into the unknown darkness.

Sagittarius the Archer:

Ruler Jupiter. Mutable Fire.

Sagittarius implies freedom of action. This is fire which seeks an outlet. Chiron is the centaur who was both hunter and healer. He was instructed by Artemis and Apollo, a reminder of which is seen in the glyph of the arrow. Artemis is the goddess who enjoys the chase, is patroness of wild animals and who invented the cat. Chiron in turn taught Asclepius (Apollo's son) the art of medicine. Medicine is also the attribute of Isis-Bastet.

Sagittarius is the hunter and the cat in this sign seeks the freedom to do so. Male cats will wander far and wide, staying away several days at a time. Hunting is still a field sport pursued by many at this time of the year.

Nearer to home, if not the home, Jupiter is a god of thunder and lightening. The oak is his tree as it is of Cat-Annis. It signifies power and strength. The cat, as protector of the home was believed to prevent damage due to the fiery elements. It is at this time of the year that the cat sits before the fire and gazes into it's soul. Jupiter signifies wisdom and ideas - just what goes through the feline brain as he stares at the flames.....?

Jupiter as ruler signifies expansiveness. He as a sky-deity brings light in the form of the dawn (he is not, however, a sun god). The full moon is also sacred to Jupiter. As fire is inspiration, Jupiter brings 'enlightenment' and knowledge.

Capricorn the Goat:

Ruler Saturn. Cardinal Earth.

The symbol of a goat with the tail of a fish is based upon the form of the Mesopotamian deity Ea or Enki. His other form is that of a man carrying a jar from which gushes water and is the symbol of the next sign, Aquarius.

Ea's name means 'House of Water', referring to the sweet water from which all life sprang. These are cosmic waters, not the salt sea. He was not originally a sun deity but was perceived as arising from the waters. In later times he had a son Marduk, who was 'Son of the Sun'; Enki then equates with Ra as the sun arising out of the primal waters of unconsciousness into being. He is god of wisdom, prophecy and is also known as 'Lord of the Sacred Eye'. His wife was Ninki, Earth goddess and Mother of All, again being similar to Isis. The birth of the sun takes place in Capricorn.

Saturn, who is these days regarded as signifying doom and gloom in astrology was originally a deity of seed. The Romans equated him with Greek Cronos. Saturn was responsible for the treasury (which links him with Pluto/Hades as guardian of wealth) and state records. His main claim to fame comes in the Saturnalia which is the forerunner of the modern Christmas. The Saturnalia belied Saturn's reputation as a misery and heralded the birth of the Sun at the winter solstice.

Much merrymaking and overturning of the social order gave rise to seven days of misrule. Many people with a strong Capricornian influence have a lively sense of humour.

The cat is one of Saturn's animals along with bats, owls, mice and serpents. All are either connected with the darkness or wisdom. Saturn brings order, responsibility and discipline to our lives. He also symbolises the ability to learn from received values (i.e. those which we acquire from others) and internal values arising from ourselves. Sooner or later we have to make a choice whether to accept or reject these.

Saturn's cat represents that dilemma. There is no escape and the sooner we learn the better we will be. Our lives will be enriched (Saturn guarded riches) by avoiding the pitfalls the undisciplined fall into. The cat also belongs to the crones Cerridwen (Mother of Wisdom) and the Cailleach Bheur, (the Blue Hag of Winter). The mother is often indicated in this house as teacher and disciplinarian of children. A female cat is an excellent disciplinarian of her kittens. Saturn also instils self-reliance. We cannot help others if we are unable to help ourselves. We must first put our own house in order.

Aquarius the Water Carrier:

Rulers Saturn and Uranus. Fixed Air.

As mentioned above, the symbol of Aquarius is the alternative of that of Ea or Enki. Aquarius is detached, humanitarian, unconventional and progressive in outlook. The mind reasons but can be dogmatic in attitude. (Never try to outstubborn a cat). The cat in this sign manages his life without consulting his feelings; he is both resourceful and unpredictable.

Aquarius makes us take responsibility for ourselves and our own well-being for only by those means can we take responsibility for the care of others. It has often been mistaken for selfishness and a cat has the reputation of 'not caring'. Which is wrong. To put it another way, if a man is drowning, there is no point in jumping in the water and drowning with him. You must learn to swim first. Puss in Boots is such a cat: he saw a need in the master who was kind to him and acted accordingly to help him.

The Japanese story of the black cat who became a geisha to repay the poor people who had cared for her while a cat is another example. The cat is independent, resourceful and intelligent. We are now leaving the Piscean age and entering that of Aquarius. Self-help groups are springing up

184

to aid those who are under addiction to drugs and alcohol or who are suicidal (Pisces).

Uranus is the son/husband of the Earth Mother, Gaia. The eldest son, Cronus, castrated him and cast the severed genitalia into the sea. The legend has much in common with the Set/Osiris myth. Unlike Osiris, however, Uranus had no cult as such and passed into oblivion. The influence of Uranus is to break down the limits to understanding which we impose upon ourselves.

Uranus rules astrology as well as the modern electronics and computer industry. Micro-surgery and ancient methods of healing offer choice. Science flourished at the same time as the planet Uranus' discovery in 1781. Uranus also marks functional changes of life in both sexes (along with the Moon and Saturn). These changes affect the endocrine system and indicate a progression into another phase (or boundary). Part of this system is the pineal gland, the 'Third Eye' of clairvoyance thought to be situated in the forehead. The cat has a reputation for clairvoyance and psychic awareness. It is thought that these abilities in man will be accepted and used for the common good in the coming age.

Pisces the Fishes:

Rulers Neptune and Jupiter. Mutable Water.

The last of the twelve signs and probably the most difficult to interpret. The symbol of this sign shows two fish swimming in the opposite direction. This represents the dual nature of the sign. In this sign, however, it is the emotions which pull both ways at once. It has been said that to argue with a Piscean is to change sides three times and still not find a solution. The essentials of the sign indicate extremes of action (like the cat).

Pisces is capable of the most self-sacrificing acts of compassion. Generosity and kindness are the by-words for this sign. Many clairvoyants and mediums are found under this sign as are saints, mystics and people who use the imagination; poets, musicians and artists. There are two cats found in this sign. The first is the cat who sits with the 'owner' whether he/she be artist or clairvoyant; often from my own experience it is as though the animal offers not only company but a psychic link which brings inspiration and insight. Many writers and artists would attest to the beneficent company of their cats.

The second cat is the sad victim of man's intolerance, cruelty and ignorance. The cat of the sacrifice, killed with no intent of cruelty, but to offer unto the gods that which they already owned. The innocent victims of the appalling witchcraft trials when the cat was the scapegoat for repression and malaise in society. People too, often cat lovers were subject to the same forces. There is the cat who sacrifices what it is for what it may become. This cat knows the power of faith.

The French story of the 'White Cat' who helps a young man to gain his inheritance is one such. After helping him as much as she can, she begs him to decapitate her in order to regain her human form. It is not the act of death which turned the cat into a woman: the woman was already within, waiting to be released by an act of love and faith.

Pisces does have a deeply spiritual quality to it, however and a tendency to transcend the material world into a place where opposites will at last harmonise and be reconciled.

CHAPTER 15

FOLK-LORE AND SUPERSTITION

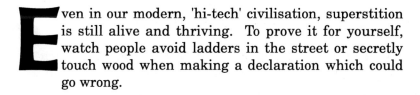ven in our modern, 'hi-tech' civilisation, superstition is still alive and thriving. To prove it for yourself, watch people avoid ladders in the street or secretly touch wood when making a declaration which could go wrong.

What is superstition? It is best defined as the remnants of an ancient ritual or belief, the reason for which is forgotten, but is still partly observed. Ask most people why stepping under a ladder is bad luck or why we touch wood and the chances are they will give a wry grin or a shrug of the shoulders and confess they do not know the reason - they just do it. They may feel silly confessing it, but they would feel very anxious if they did not avoid the ladder or forgot to touch wood. A superstition is a safeguard against the vagaries of the unknown and the unseen. We should never laugh at those who believe in these rituals - the psychological impact of an omission can be devastating to the person concerned. Ask any sportsperson about the loss of a mascot/favourite pair of socks/or whatever.

Much of the superstitious rituals described below can be traced back to earlier times and a reason given for them.

Of all animals, the cat has attracted more superstition to itself than any other. Nor is there any consensus of opinion: it all depends on where you live: not only do nations differ in their beliefs, but smaller areas within those countries offer conflicting advice. So let us take a look at the superstition surrounding our feline friend, beginning with that all-time favourite, the black cat.

The Black Cat

> Whenever the cat of the house is black,
> The lasses of lovers will have no lack.

The black cat was the alleged form of Satan and the witch's familiar; (most illustrations of the witch show her with a black cat, but her companion is often of another colour as well). Black is darkness, secrecy and mystery. Opinion is mixed as to whether the black cat is lucky or unlucky. It is a matter of geography, ownership and what the cat is doing at the time.

To own a black cat is considered lucky.

To meet a black cat which turns away from you is unlucky.

A black cat which crosses your path is unlucky.

To turn a black cat out of the house or chase one away is unlucky.

It is lucky to receive a postcard with a black cat on it.

It is lucky to keep or touch the fur of a black cat.

It is lucky to wear black cat charms and brooches.

During the period between the two World Wars, black cat teapots were popular.

The White Cat

The white cat should, by it's opposite colour to the black cat, fare better in man's estimation. This is not always so: The white cat has also been thought of as the Devil incarnate.

Other Colours

The tabby cat is notorious as a witch's familiar:

'Thrice the brinded cat hath mewed'

Shakespeare: Macbeth.

A tortoiseshell cat is said to confer clairvoyance on it's owner.

Sailors and Fishermen

It is not surprising, considering the unpredictable nature of the seas, that sailors and fishermen need all the protection they can get. The sea can be a harsh mistress, ruled by the moon and having much in common with the changeability of the sign Pisces. (Actors, those who easily shed one role and slip into another, also have a strong affinity with this sign). You never really know where you are with Pisces.

Seamen are generally kind to cats. Cats bring luck to any vessel they board and are considered infallible weather-forecasters.

In the days of sail, progress was entirely dependent on the wind, or lack of it. During the witchcraft trials of the seventeenth century, many were accused of raising storms. The favourite method being to throw a black cat into the sea. It was therefore taboo for a sailor to throw a cat overboard. To prevent storms, the ship's cat would be placed under a barrel or tub, presumably to prevent its being washed away.

This method worked on land as well as sea: sailors' wives would keep a black cat at home to put beneath a tub to either becalm his vessel and prevent him going to sea or to bring him safely home by preventing storms. Sailors waiting for a favourable wind would believe that someone had put a cat under a tub.

A sailor on his way to his ship would return home if he met a cat which crossed his path. If a black cat ran before him, it was considered a good omen for the voyage.

In Aberdeen, a poor catch of fish was said to be due to 'meeting the cat in the morning'. In the Orkney and Shetland Isles, to mention the word 'cat' while setting the lines was forbidden. Other words were used instead: kirser, fitting, vengla or foodin.

In several languages the word for 'cat' has nautical associations. In English a small boat is called a 'cat' (see notes on Dick Whittington). Rigging is the 'cat-rig', the anchor is supported on a beam known as the 'cat-head' and to hang the anchor on it is 'catting' the anchor. A light breeze is a 'cat's paw'.

190

Actors

Like the seafarers above, acting is a hazardous profession. Not perhaps from the wrath of the elements, but from the uncertainty of work, opportunity and public opinion. Actors tend to like cats, using as they do much of the feminine side of the personality. Many theatres keep an in-house cat, Drury Lane had Amrose, The Garrick was home to Bouncer and The Adelphi was graced by a brother and sister team known as Plug and Socket. The only taboo the acting profession have concerning the cat is that it is very bad luck if a cat runs across the stage during a performance.

Miners

A profession as dangerous and unpredictable as seamanship. Mining comes under the rulership of Saturn and the cat is one of Saturn's animals. There appear to be few superstitions concerning the cat in the mining industry, but those we have coincide with those of the sailors. If a black cat crossed the path of a miner on his way to the pit, he would return home. In lean times, a cat would be shut in a cold oven until a seam of coal was drawn. Cornish miners would refuse to work on a level if a cat was seen there - the cat had to be killed first.

Updates

A case of an old superstitions finding a new life: Motorists and drivers have adopted this one. If a black cat crosses in front of the vehicle from left to right, it warns of a puncture (or, Heaven forbid, a deceased pussy).

Football teams have been known to take a black cat onto the football pitch with them.

House and Home

The Weather-Forecaster

Before the days of the Met. Office, the cat was regarded as a forecaster par excellence. Scrutinising puss before making a journey, harvesting or doing the week's washing was a must to avoid disaster.

In Lapland, folk watch the antics of the cat before setting out on a journey.

Storms

In addition to the sailors' lore there is the following: In Scotland, a cat which scratches a chair or table leg is thought to be 'raising a wind'.

A Slavic belief was that during thunderstorms, the bodies of the household cats are possessed by devils. Every time there is a clap of thunder, angels pray to God and the devils mock them. The cats are then cleared from the house as the angels, taking offence, hurl fire (lightening) at the devils within the cats which could burn the house down.

To calm a storm in Ireland, a cat is put under a metal pot until the weather eases. This is an interesting addition to the maritime method. If the pot is made of iron, this is believed to nullify all magical workings. In this case it is thought that the cat itself is the worker of magic. A witch in disguise?

The Cat as Healing Agent

The cat has been used in 'medicinal' potions for hundreds, if not thousands of years. Most of the recipes are unpleasant and are only included here for the sake of completeness and to illustrate the extent of man's desperation or ghastly ingenuity when ill. The two important parts of the cat's person were the eyes and the tail. The cat's occult power was believed to be at it's strongest in these organs. There is a Japanese belief that a (live) black cat can cure spasms if placed on the patient's stomach, the same is thought to ease melancholia and epilepsy. (I have personal experience that a cat can ease griping and spasms in the stomach, simply by curling up on the affected part. A remedy I have been grateful for many times in the past. The cat placed herself there of her own volition). For tension, stress, loneliness, fear and heart problems, the companionship of a beloved cat purring gently cannot be bettered.

The Eye

Eye Complaints

Blindness: In parts of Scotland, it was believed that mental blindness, delusion or confusion could be cured by 'casting the cat over...' This presumably means to throw or swing a cat over the head of the afflicted.

The seventeenth century naturalist, E. Topsell gives the following advice.

'Take the head of a black cat, which hath not a spot of any other colour in it and burn to powder in an earthen pot, leaded or glazed within. Then take this powder and through a quill blow it thrice a day into thy eye. And if in the night any heat do thereby annoy thee, take two leaves of an oke, wet with cold water, and bind them to the eye, so shall all pain flie away and blindness depart. Although it hath oppressed thee a whole year...'

The Tale of a Tail

As an all-round preventative of sickness in the family, cut off a black cat's tail and bury it under the doorstep.

Styes: An English remedy for relief of styes was to rub the stye with a tom-cat's tail.

From Northamptonshire, take a single hair from the tip of a black cat's tail on the first night of the new moon. Draw it nine times across the swollen eyelid. This cure must be very old: the cure would presumably work with the increase of the moon and be completed with the full moon. Nine is the number of the triple moon Goddess.

Cornwall offers this for relief: Stroke the eye with the tail of a black cat, saying:

'I poke thee, I don't poke thee. I toke the queff that's under the 'ee, oh, qualy way; oh qualy way.

Irritation or Rash: A left-handed man must find a black cat and whirl it around his head three times. An ointment is then prepared from nine drops of blood from the cat's tail and mixed with the charred remains of nine barley-corns.

This is applied with a golden wedding ring as you walk three times around the patient backwards, invoking the Trinity. This is another very old cure. Barley is a cooling herb so it's inclusion in this cure is obvious. To walk backwards is to 'undo' or regress a situation. Nine drops and nine barley corns all connect with the Goddess. Which Trinity is being invoked is open to debate.

Shingles: Apply fresh blood from a black cat's tail over the entire affected area.

Whitlows: Pass the tail of a black cat from the back of the hand between the first and second fingers, up between second and third fingers then back down between third and fourth fingers. Do this on three successive nights.

Warts: This can only be effective during the month of May - Rub the wart with the tail of a tortoiseshell tom-cat. Perhaps the incidence of male torties was greater then than now. I can remember a Botany lecturer who, at the beginning of each college year asked his new students whether any of them owned a tortoiseshell tom-cat. Nobody ever did. They are rare.

TO DETER anyone of thinking to utilise the above, the Celts believed that if you trod on (or otherwise damaged) a cat's tail, a serpent would appear and sting you!!!!!!!!!!!!!

Catskin

Cat fur has many uses. One is as a remedy for burns and it is still believed to be effective in the treatment of rheumatism, sore throats and hives.

Inflammation: A Dutch remedy was to apply the skin of a freshly killed cat.

The May Cat

Kittens born during the month of May are (or were) considered very unlucky and poor mousers. In addition, they were believed to bring snakes and slow worms in the house.

The reason for this is not clear, but the wild cat of Scotland has only one litter a year and that during May. Perhaps someone attempted to domesticate one of these kittens and found them to be unsuited for the purpose. Another explanation may be linked with the Beltane ceremony, which takes place on 30th. April. This festival is a fire-festival, to encourage the sun and growth of crops. Goddesses connected with May are sometimes kindly but a few (like Cardea) are dangerous. Hence it is inviting trouble to bring her sacred flower, the hawthorn into the house. She is an enemy to children and will surely follow it indoors.

Cat Charms

Cat charms made with whiskers can bring bad luck, disease and death to the victim.

Black cat charms and brooches are worn.

In the twenties and thirties black cat teapots were popular.

Loyalty

Loyalty is placed in the chapter on superstition because many people do not believe that cats possess it. Rubbish! Below are two accounts of a cat's care for her imprisoned 'master' at a time when cats were persecuted mercilessly.

In the year 1483, Sir Henry Wyatt was thrown into the Tower of London because he voiced doubts about King Richard III's claim to the throne. The punishment was particularly cruel because he was left to die of cold and starvation.

He was saved by a cat, 'God sent a cat to feed and warm him'. The cat kept him alive by catching pigeons, which were cooked for him by the jailer. At night Sir Henry slept curled up with his feline friend. There is a memorial to the cat in the Church, Boxley, Kent.

Henry Wriothesley, Earl of Southampton was accused of plotting against Queen Elizabeth I and thrown into prison in the Tower of London. A few weeks later he was joined by his cat, Trixie. Trixie had made her way from the south coast, a journey of some one hundred miles, climbed down a chimney and was reunited with her 'master'. Sir Henry was released in 1603, on the death of the Queen. There is a portrait of them both in the possession of the Duke of Buccleuch.

INDEX

Breton, 46, 103
bridge, 125
Britain, 19, 23, 51, 59, 65, 69, 84, 99, 101, 108-109, 115, 117, 122, 125, 127
Bubastis, 10, 12, 15, 24, 81, 128
Buddha, 46, 88, 104, 132
Burma, 87-89

cactus cat, 162
Cailleach Bheur, 66, 114, 184
Cairbre Cinn-cait, 111, 166
Cait Sith, 115
Cambyses II, 9
Cancer, 55, 174-176
Canon Episcopi, 52, 141, 146
Capalu, 119
Capricorn, 63, 182-183
Cardinal Richelieu, 148
Cardinal Wolsey, 148
Cat-Headed Men, 165
cat o' nine tails, 78
Cat of Lapis Lazuli, 78
cat's cradle, 130, 176
Cath Palug, 65, 69, 115, 117-118
Cathars, 45, 133, 141
catskin, 111, 116, 137, 159, 166, 195
catspaw, 125, 153
Cattle, 2, 8, 63, 102-103
Ccoa, 162
Celtic Christianity, 122

Celtic, 41, 59, 65, 69, 76, 80-81, 83, 90, 100, 108, 110-111, 119-120, 122, 127, 166, 169, 171, 180
Ceres, 53, 63, 179
Cerridwen, 53, 65, 110, 115-117, 184
Charles I, 176
Cheshire cat, 163
China, 87, 90-91, 95, 177
Chiron, 166, 181-182
Christianity, 5, 54, 80, 115, 122, 143
Church, 44, 52, 59, 100, 104, 122-123, 125, 127-128, 131-135, 137, 141-144, 197
Cinderella, 157, 159
Clogh-magh-righ-cat, 111
Coatlicue, 46
Copts, 45
corn spirit, 63
cow, 24, 27-28, 35, 112
crone, 55, 136, 180
Cuchulainn, 110-111

Delphic Oracle, 41
Demeter, 40, 53, 57, 59, 63-65, 67, 78, 86, 177
Dermot, 46, 83, 113
Devil, 2-3, 44, 46, 80, 98, 105, 120, 125, 128, 130, 132, 134, 137, 141-142, 146, 180, 189
Diana, 9, 24, 35, 51-52, 82, 86, 109, 141-143, 145, 180

A selection of other Capall Bann titles - free catalogue available

Cats' Company
A book of cats & - history - reincarnation - healing - communication - stories
By Ann Walker
Ann explores the role of the cat through history, from being worshipped in Ancient Egypt to being cruelly treated and hated in Medieval Europe. The book includes tales of cats who returned to their owners after death, both in spirit and reincarnated form. Stating that "The Ancient Celts believed that the eyes of a cat were windows through which humans could explore the inner world", we are given an extract from a grimoire giving guidance on how to attune yourself to your cat. Believing in the healing power of cats and our ability to think/talk with them, Ann shares many stories of the cats she has known and loved over the years. A fascinating and enthralling book for cat lovers everywhere. ISBN 1 898307 32 6   £10.95

Your Talking Pet by Ann Walker
Your Talking Pet is about 'companion animals', the cats and dogs who live in our houses and are called 'pets'. For various reasons, we selected these two species to share our homes and our lives and the result is a mutual dependency; they on us for their well-being, we on them for companionship, love and even to boost our self esteem. Sometimes there is a total misunderstanding between us, at others we share a bond that is as strong as any we have with our own kind. Packed with interesting facts and real-life stories, some funny and some sad, this book about people and pets will strike a chord in the heart of everyone who has ever lived with, and loved, a cat or a dog. ISBN 1898307 873   £8.95

Psychic Animals - A fascinating investigation of paranormal behaviour
By Dennis Bardens Foreword by David Bellamy
".......remarkably interesting & totally 'different' book on the mysterious powers displayed by animals of all kinds........those who read it will find themselves observing animals, & perhaps themselves too, in an entirely new light." David Bellamy
For centuries animals of all kinds have displayed amazing powers of psychic intelligence as bizarre & inexplicable as the strangest human paranormal experiences. Fascinating accounts of unusual animal behaviour include the stories of the horse that helped police locate the body of a murdered baby, the stowaway dog that sailed 5,000 miles to find his master & the seagull that sought help for an injured woman. In this unique study, internationally known psychic investigator Dennis Bardens presents a persuasive body of evidence revealing & explaining remarkable feats of animal telepathy, precognition & long-distance perception. ISBN 1 898307 39 3   £10.95

The Mystic Life of Animals   by Ann Walker
As the New Age moves upon us, we will increasingly recognise animals as spiritual beings worthy of our respect. "Communication is the golden key that unlocks the door to understanding." Animal communication is mostly concerned with emotions, feelings, events and happenings in the here and now. We tend to think that animal communication involves them understanding what we want, but in truth, it is a two-way process. A lifetime of living with and loving animals has led Ann Walker to conclude that much communication with animals is on a mind to mind level, and she tells of many personal psychic experiences with animals. Old superstitions and magical beliefs about animals are examined, also the attitude of different religions. Ann shares her own experiences and those of others with dead pets returning or sending messages and expresses a firm belief in the continued spiritual existence of animals after death.
ISBN 1861630166   £7.95

Sacred Celtic Animals by Marion Davies

Animals affected the everyday lives of the Celts. The Celts saw animals as representations, representatives and messengers of their deities. They took animal names for themselves and their tribes and saw portents and auguries in animals' movements and behaviour. Animals featured extensively in Celtic legends and decorated their weapons, houses and accoutrements. Celtic shamans linked with animals and their warriors and hunters invoked the power of totem animals to help in their endeavours. This book details the myths, legends and correspondences linking the Celts and the animal world. Brilliantly illustrated by Simon Rouse.
ISBN 1898307 75X   £11.95

Lore of the Sacred Horse - The Magical Lore of Horses
by Marion Davies

This noble animal has been food & transport, the innocent participant in Man's wars, at one time his Deity & the honoured companion of his Deities. The symbol of majesty & power. From seed-time to harvest, the horse has been at the forefront of agricultural economy. Even so, Man's faithful servant has known the full extent of cruelty & ingratitude, may the Gods forgive us. This book traces this relationship from earliest times, stressing the religio-magical aspects. The Sacred Horse is rooted deep within our race-memory & is still to be found in our high-tech culture. Topics covered include: Horse Magic, Horse Cults, Horse Whisperers, Secret Societies, The Hobby Horse - Ancient Horse Festivals & Celebrations, Superstition & Folklore, Toadmen & more.
ISBN 1898307 17 2   £10.95

Wondrous Land - The Faery Faith of Ireland by Kay Mullin

Dr Kay Mullin, a clinical psychologist by profession, was introduced to the world of faery by spirit channelled through a medium. That meeting led to extensive research in Ireland, collecting stories both old and new - from people who not only know of faeries, but see them too - in the land so long associated with them. The result is this wonderful book. The text is complemented with lyrical poetry from an Irish seer, and exquisite drawings. The faery faith is real, alive and growing in Ireland.
ISBN 186163 010 7   £10.95   R97   Illustrated

Handbook of Fairies   by Ronan Coghlan

Many theories have been put forward about fairies - whether their origins are the deities of pre-Christian religions, primitive peoples driven into hiding, or even the denizens of UFOs.This is a detailed guide to fairies and other otherworldly beings. The different types of fairy and other otherworld beings are described, together with stories and legends about them. The possible origins of fairies are also discussed as are various theories about them, their links or differences from aliens, the passing of time in the Otherworld and other fascinating topics. When we consider the realm of Faerie, we should hesitate to attribute it to the mere superstition of our ancestors, on whom we are encouraged to shower unmerited contempt by a world-view which tells us we are constantly making what it terms "progress".
ISBN 186163 042 5   £9.95

Auguries & Omens - The Magical Lore of Birds   by Yvonne Aburrow

Examines in detail the interpretation of birds as auguries & omens, the mythology of birds (Roman, Greek, Celtic & Teutonic), the folklore & weather lore associated with them, their use in heraldry & falconry & their appearances in folk songs & poetry. The book explores these areas in a general way, then goes into specific details of individual birds from the albatross to the yellowhammer, including exotic & even mythical birds.
ISBN 1898307 113   £10.95